Right From the Start

Right From the Start

A Guide to Nourishing the Spirit-Born Life

by
Krista Graham

WESTBOW
PRESS®
A DIVISION OF THOMAS NELSON
& ZONDERVAN

Scripture quotations taken from the New American Standard Bible®,
Copyright © 1960, 1962, 1963, 1968, 1971, 1972, 1973,
1975, 1977, 1995 by The Lockman Foundation
Used by permission. (www.Lockman.org)

Scripture taken from the Holman Christian Standard Bible ®
Copyright © 2003, 2002, 2000, 1999 by Holman Bible Publishers. All rights reserved.

WestBow Press books may be ordered through booksellers or by contacting:

WestBow Press
A Division of Thomas Nelson & Zondervan
1663 Liberty Drive
Bloomington, IN 47403
www.westbowpress.com
1 (866) 928-1240

ISBN: 978-1-5127-0163-0 (sc)
ISBN: 978-1-5127-0164-7 (e)

Print information available on the last page.

WestBow Press rev. date: 01/06/2016

For Brittany

Table of Contents

Acknowledgements

This book would not have been possible without the support and encouragement of my husband and five children. If they had not given me the freedom to spend countless hours in studying, writing, and revising, this book would still be a pile of lists and notes in a basket on my desk. I also deeply appreciate the wise input of Sue Towle, the blue editing pencil and vast Bible knowledge of Scott Palmer, and the insightful field testing skills of Connie Zobel. Each of them was indispensable to this project.

Part One

Right From the Start

Nourishing the Spirit-Born Life

Introduction

This Bible study is designed for two groups of people. First, it is for new Christians who are just beginning their life with God. These are the people who are saying to themselves, *"I want to get this right from the start."*

But this study is also for a second group. It is for people like me, who have known the Lord for decades yet somehow feel *they did not get it right from the start.* It is for those of us who want to go back and lay a new foundation so we can move forward in a new way, hoping the second half of our lives with God will be better than the first.

So whether you are new to the Lord or looking for a fresh start, I pray that God will speak to you through this study and put you on solid footing in your walk with Him. In the words of A.W. Tozer , "As long as Christ sits on the mediatorial throne, every day is a good day and all days are the day of salvation." Begin a new day with me. And this time, let's get it right from the start!

Lesson One

What is a Christian?
The Nature of the Spirit-Born Life

In our family, we've never had much luck in caring for living things. For example, my mother is famous for killing plants. She has drowned cacti, baked shade-loving plants in sunny windows, and killed sun-loving plants in shady corners. Over the years, we have poisoned fish with chlorinated tap water. We have killed birds by feeding them pellets instead of seeds. (That really wasn't our fault...Long story.) We have killed rose bushes by over-pruning and blueberry bushes by under-pruning.

What do all of the above have in common? Ignorance. All the damage done was a result of not understanding a living thing and not knowing how to care for it.

So what does this have to do with living the Christian life?

The Christian life is just that – a life. It is a living thing, and living things need to be cared for in a certain way. Once we have come to know Christ, we have eternal life. We can't lose our salvation. But we can render ourselves as good as dead – unproductive and unfruitful for God. If we are not careful, our ignorance or misunderstanding of the nature of our new life can stop our progress before it gets started. We can set ourselves up for decades of frustration and failure rather than vibrant growth and progress.

What is a Christian?

Let's start with a test. Answer the following true or false:

_____ A person is a Christian if he or she believes the right things about God and Jesus. (Jesus was born of a virgin, died on the cross, rose from the dead, etc.)

_____ A person is a Christian if he or she obeys God's laws. (keep the 10 commandments, or love God with all their heart and love their neighbor as themselves)

If the first is true, then Christianity is a creed. It is agreeing to a statement of facts about Jesus. Let's see if this is all it takes to be a Christian.

Read James 2:19. (When James says, "You believe God is one..." he is referring to a classic doctrinal statement that all Jews would have known at that time. So understand that as a reference to just believing the truth about God or believing what the Bible teaches.)

Who "also believes" the truth about God?

According to this verse, does believing a list of true statements about God and Jesus make a person a Christian?

If just knowing facts about Jesus doesn't make you a Christian, what about obedience to the Law? Read Luke 18:18-23.

This young man had kept the Law as perfectly as any person could. Is this enough for Jesus?

Read Galatians 3:11.
Can anyone be justified (saved, made right with God) through keeping the Law?

If believing facts alone doesn't make you a Christian (because even the demons believe in God) and if living a good life alone doesn't make you a Christian (because even proud Pharisees can keep the letter of the law), then what exactly DOES make you a Christian?

Two Word Pictures

God is very gracious to us in the way He explains things to us. He knows that spiritual truths can be hard for our human minds to grasp, so He puts things in terms we can understand. In explaining how a person becomes a Christian, God uses two very familiar word pictures: babies and plants.

Picture #1: Conception and Birth

Read John 3:1-8.
In verse 6, Jesus describes two kinds of life in this passage: _____ (physical life which we get when we are born physically) and _____(the kind of life that begins when we are "born AGAIN" , or born spiritually).

Jesus explains to Nicodemus that he must have a second kind of birth that will bring to life a part of him that is not alive right now: his spirit. Just like his physical life began with physical birth, his spiritual life must begin with a spiritual birth.

This matter of spiritual birth and life is very important. It is what makes Christianity different from any other religion.

Turn the page in your Bible to John 4.
In John 3 (which you read above) Jesus was talking to a religious leader. Nicodemus would have been to people in his time much like a pastor of a church is to us in our time. He was a religious leader and a Bible teacher. In John 4, we have pretty much the opposite. The woman that Jesus is speaking to in this chapter has been divorced five times and now she is living with a man she is not married to. She knows very little about religion. All she is sure of is that she is on the outside of whatever true religion might be.

Read John 4:7-26.
There are a few things going on in this passage.
First, Jesus is offering her something. What is it? (verse 13-14)

What does she think he means by "living water"? (v.15)

To find out exactly what Jesus is offering her, turn to John 7:37-39. In this passage, Jesus is talking to a crowd and giving them the same offer he gave the woman at the well: Living water. But John tells us exactly what that "living water" is. What is it? (v.39)

Turn back to John 4.

In verse 20, the woman asks a question about worshipping on mountains which, in our day, would basically be like asking Jesus this question: "I have heard different people claim this church or that church is the only place to find God. Which church is the right one?"

In verse 23-24, Jesus explains to her that the question isn't so much "which church should I go to" as it is, "Do I have what it takes to be able to worship God at all?" He is telling the woman much the same thing that He told Nicodemus: God is a spiritual Being. To worship Him, you must be spiritually alive.

The metaphor of Spiritual birth and life tells us that a Christian is one who has been born again. A Christian is spiritually alive and is able to worship God because of that.

What exactly is "spiritual birth"?

In John 3, Jesus implied to Nicodemus that the way spiritual birth comes about is similar to the way that physical birth comes about. So, let's examine that picture more closely.

When a new life is conceived, there are two parents involved. Both contribute something. The mother's contribution is simply a cell. We call it an egg. As we all know, an egg contains the potential for life; but it will not, on its own, ever grow into a living thing. Perhaps every child goes through a stage where they think the chicken eggs in the fridge, if left alone long enough, will eventually hatch into chicks. I think most parents dread that awkward day when they have to explain to their children why this is not so. By God's miraculous design, the father's contribution is that which makes the egg into a new individual – a living soul.

In exactly the same way, a human being will never become spiritually alive unless something external to ourselves is introduced – something that turns the non-living potential for spiritual life within us into something that is alive and altogether new.

The Human Spirit

According to Ephesians 2:1-5, what spiritual condition are we born in, as human beings? (see v.1 & 5)

Romans 5:12-21 explains clearly how we all came to be born physically alive but with a dead spirit. Adam's sin brought spiritual death to the entire human race. Because of Adam's sin, we are born dead to God and alive to sin in our very nature. The human spirit is like a candle wick – dark and cold, waiting for a flame to set it alight. Or, as in the birth metaphor Jesus uses, like an unfertilized egg, awaiting the infusion of life from outside itself.

The Spirit of Life

According to Romans 8:9, what does every single Christian have?

Paul wrote the book of Romans. His favorite term for the Holy Spirit is "the Spirit of Christ." John wrote the book of John, obviously. But he also wrote the letters called 1, 2, and 3 John at the end of the

New Testament. John carries the same imagery he wrote with in John 3 into the letter of 1 John when he describes the Holy Spirit.

Read 1 John 2:29-3:9. (Be sure you are looking at the letter of FIRST John, not the Gospel of John.) Notice the repeated references to being "born of God."
In 3:1, what does John say we are?

In 3:9, John says no one who is born of God sins (meaning constantly, habitually sinning as the "norm" of our lives). What reason does he give for this new kind of life that does not sin?

…"God's _____ abides in him."

The Greek word here for "seed" is *sperma*. You don't have to be a biology major to guess what the English word equivalent would be. John is using the same metaphor of conception to describe the "birth" of our new, spiritual nature that Jesus was hinting at in John 3 when he talked with Nicodemus. He emphasizes the presence of the Holy Spirit indwelling the believer repeatedly in First John (see 2:20, 2:27, 3:24, 4:4, 4:13, 4:16, 5:7, 5:10, 12).

A Christian is one whose spirit has been re-born, born of God, born from above. This happens when God's Holy Spirit enters into us and indwells our human spirit. This is where we get the terminology of Jesus "coming into our heart" as a way of describing the moment of becoming a Christian. God's Spirit enters into us and we become alive to God. We become capable of relating to God, who is a Spirit and must be known spiritually.

First John 5:1-5 explains that believing the right facts about Jesus and living in obedience to Jesus are both part of BEING a Christian; but they are not the definition of a Christian. A Christian is a person who has been born again – brought to new life by the presence of God's Spirit within them. That is what makes our faith different from the belief of the demons and makes our obedience different from the legalism of the Pharisees.

To summarize, the word picture of spiritual conception and new birth teaches us the following:
- Human beings have two aspects to their nature: physical and spiritual (John 3:6)
- Human beings are born spiritually dead, incapable of knowing God (Romans 5:12 & John 4:24)
- If we believe in Jesus as our savior, we become "born of God." (1 John 5:1) We begin a life as a person who is alive to God.
- Salvation is a moment of spiritual conception where a new life is begun by God's Spirit entering into our spirit and bringing His life to our dead spirits. No Holy Spirit = no spiritual life. (Romans 8:9)
- God's Holy Spirit actually lives in our physical bodies. He dwells in us. Literally. (1 Cor. 6:19)

Later we will study the implications of this word picture to how we grow and mature in our new spiritual life, but for now we are just concerned with defining the Christian life in how it begins.

So, let's turn to Jesus' second word picture for how a person passes from spiritual death to spiritual life: the plant.

Picture #2: Seeds, Soil, and Plants

The picture of the baby emphasizes the role of the Holy Spirit in our salvation. The picture of the plant emphasizes the role of God's Word. In First John 3:9, we saw that the seed of God abiding in a believer was a reference to the Holy Spirit. In Matthew 13, we are going to see the seed used as a reference to God's Word. After we examine this second word picture, we will look at why mixing the metaphors of Spirit and Word is not a contradiction, but rather a key truth in itself that we need to grasp.

Read Luke 8:4-8.
Then read Luke 8:9-15.
In the second passage, you will see that Jesus is explaining the symbolism of the story He told in the first passage. This is a rare treat for the Bible student – to have the explanation of a lesson spelled out plainly for us so that there is no chance of misunderstanding the point.

What is the seed?

What is the soil? (see v.12,15)

Notice the same seed is sown in each case, but the outcome varies based on what kind of soil the seed lands on. The parable is about how people respond to the Word of God – whether they receive it or not. But the different soils (hearts) are not the focus of this study. What matters to us is that the seed (the Word of God) is meant to take root in the heart and produce a fruitful plant.

James 1:18 describes a person becoming a Christian in terms of being "brought forth" (given life) by the Word of truth to be first fruits – an early crop for Him.
James 1:21 tells us to receive the _____ implanted which is able to save our souls.

The Word of God enters the heart like a seed enters soil. When that seed (the Word of God) is received with faith, it sprouts to life. (Romans 10:17) The life is not in the soil; it is in the seed. The seed germinates sprouts, grows, and produces fruit. This is the picture of salvation using the seed metaphor.

As in First John 5, we also see in James 1:22 that obedience is the result of new life – not the cause of it. A person who hears the Word of God without believing it and acting upon it is like the soil in Jesus' story where the seed can't sink in and grow.

Why does it Matter?

Does all this matter? Do we really need to understand all the spiritual how's and why's? Can't we just believe in Jesus and live the life? Good question. And the answer is, yes, it does matter.

If we think the Christian life is just about knowing the right things and believing them, then we are going to think we grow by learning more things. We are going to think reading books and taking classes will make us better Christians. **We are going to try to grow by the strength of our own minds.**

If we think the Christian life is just about following God's rules, then we are going to think we grow by rule-keeping. We are going to set ever-higher standards for our lifestyle and think ***that we grow by our own willpower.***

The Bible warns us about following our "inflated fleshly minds." (Col. 2:18) There is a danger to accumulating spiritual knowledge for the wrong reasons. It makes us proud and less able to grow in Christ. (1 Cor. 8:1) The Bible also warns us against thinking that keeping rules will bring us closer to God. (Col. 2:20-23) Increasing in the knowledge of God is very important to our Christian life, and we are supposed to live a holy life of obedience to God. But there are two ways of doing this: the way of the flesh (our old, sinful, fallen nature) and the way of the spirit (our newly born spiritual nature).

Remember the illustration we began this lesson with -- about the plants and pets that my family has killed off over the years? Ignorance of what living things need to grow and thrive causes those living things to wither and die. Our Christian life is not just about ideas or actions. It is a living thing – a new creation, a spiritual person that is our new Self. ***If we want that inner person of the heart to thrive and grow in this God-begotten life, we need to understand what that new nature is made of and what it needs.***

That is what we are going to learn together in the weeks ahead.

Jesus said it best:

"It is the Spirit who gives life; the flesh profits nothing; the words I have spoken to you are spirit and are life." John 6:63

Lesson Two

Created for His Glory; Saved for His Love

In lesson one, we saw that God performed a miracle in allowing us to begin a new spiritual kind of life. He has given us of Himself -- His own Spirit -- and has begotten us as spiritual children. Before we go any further in this study, I think we should pause and ask ourselves *why*? Why would a God who is so magnificent, so far beyond us, stoop to do so much for us?

On the human level, we rarely go to a great deal of trouble for someone unless we have something to gain from it. So, what does God have to gain? What could possibly have motivated God to do all that He has done in relation to us?

Created for His Glory

Psalm 19:1 says, "The heavens are telling of the glory of God; and their expanse is declaring the work of His hands." God made the earth for His glory. This means that He made the earth (and the entire universe) in order to display what He is like. His creation explains much about His character, and that brings Him glory.

Read Romans 1:20. What things are clearly seen and understood through the things that God has made?

Not only did God create the heavens and the earth to bring Him glory, He also created people to bring Him glory. Like the rest of creation, we do that by displaying His attributes.

Read Genesis 1:26-27. What does this tell us about how God made man and woman? What was His design?

This is an important starting place. God made everything to bring Him glory -- to allow Him a means of displaying what He is like. In creation we see His immensity, His power, His wisdom, His orderliness, His creativity, and much more. In ourselves, we see His image because we have an ability to think and communicate, create, and appreciate beauty, organize and rule and enjoy. We have language and thought at a level that no other creatures have, so that allows us to demonstrate parts of God's character that the trees and mountains and oceans can't.

Many people ask the question, "If God made everything good, why did He allow evil to enter the world?" Or they ask, "If God has the power to stop sin and evil, why doesn't He?" These questions make sense to us from a strictly human point of view. If we had the power to make life easier for ourselves or our loved ones, we would do it. So, why doesn't God? God is so much higher than us we can't pretend to explain Him. But there is one thing we can grasp, if we are willing to do so, which does answer many of these types of questions: God is committed to something much bigger than our comfort or even our happiness. He is committed to His own glory. By allowing evil to enter the world, God's goodness suddenly showed up in high definition. By having a dark contrast to God's light, His light was all the brighter. By introducing the Liar, Satan, God's truth showed up more powerfully. Not only this, but if man had never been allowed to choose to sin, many aspects of God's character would never have been made known to us. How would we ever have known what grace, mercy, forgiveness, justice, and compassion were if there had never been an occasion for God to extend these to His people?

The best good God could give to human beings was the chance to know Him in the full spectrum of His attributes. To make all these qualities visible, there had to be sin and evil -- a contrast to His holiness and righteousness.

Now we can see not only why God created us (to bring Him glory by the ways that we bear His image) but also why He allowed sin and suffering (that we could know His nature more completely). This understanding is an important starting point for the Christian life because it puts God at the very center of everything, which is where He belongs. If we think God made the universe to serve man and make man happy, we will not be able to know Him as He wants to be known. But if we can accept that God created all things, including us, first and foremost for Himself and His glory, that is a foundation we can build on as we learn to walk with God.

God's Great Motivator

The second question we want to answer is this: Why did God save us? Why not be content to show Himself in all His glory and then destroy us in His perfect holy justice? Why go to all the trouble of sacrificing His Son? Why give us new birth and put His Spirit in us?

Read the following verses and write down both what God DID and what motivated God to act.
* Deuteronomy 7:8

* Jeremiah 31:3

* John 3:16

* Romans 5:8

* Ephesians 2:4-5

* 1 John 3:1

Read 1 John 4:8 and fill in the blank:
God is _____.

The kind of love God has is not just a feeling. It is not the weak romantic kind of love that we often think of -- a love that changes its mind or goes away with time. God's love is, next to His holiness, His most defining characteristic. God IS love. This means that every act of God is motivated by His love.

God loves His own glory and God loves people. In order to be faithful to His own good character, yet still allow Himself to be in a relationship with people, He devised the plan of sacrificing Himself in Jesus to save us and purify us from all our sin so we could be with Him forever.

The Wonder of Relationship

The biggest wonder of God's love in my mind is the fact that God so deeply desires to be in a relationship with Man. Even though He is totally complete and sufficient in Himself, God has been going far out of His way to be near Man ever since the day He created Adam and Eve.

The Timeline of God's Presence

Read Genesis 3:8-9. What was God in the habit of doing?

Read Leviticus 26:11. What does God intend to do?

Read 1 Kings 8:10-13. How does God respond when Solomon builds a temple for Him?

Read Matthew 1:23. This verse mentions one of the names Jesus would be called in the Bible: Immanuel. What does this name mean?

Read John 17:23-24. List a few of the things Jesus prays for.

In Matthew 28:18-20, Jesus is preparing to return to Heaven. What does He promise His disciples?

Read 1 Corinthians 6:19. How does God dwell with us now?

Read Revelation 21:3. Where is God going to dwell for all eternity?

In each of these verses, we see God deliberately devising a way by which He can dwell near His people.

He walked in the Garden with Adam and Eve each evening until they sinned and He had to send them away.

He provided a tabernacle (a tent dwelling) where His presence would dwell, in the form of a pillar of smoke or fire, right in the center of the Israelite's camp. There He would be surrounded by the twelve tribes of His chosen people. They would have to bring animal sacrifices to cover their sins, but He would accept those sacrifices and allow them to approach Him and to see the evidence of His nearness in the form of the cloud that hovered over the tent.

After Israel was settled in the Promised Land, King Solomon built a more permanent temple. God would continue to dwell there in Jerusalem, with His presence symbolically located on the Ark of the Covenant.

Over the years, God's people turned away from Him. They stopped coming to the temple and worshipping Him. Instead they built shrines to all kinds of idols and worshipped them instead. God had to withdraw from His people again. He could not locate Himself in the midst of idol worshippers. He disciplined His people by allowing enemies to invade them. The temple was destroyed and the ark stolen away. But it was just a golden box by that time. God's glorious presence had left long before.

Several hundred years passed and God seemed silent and distant. Then, in His most fantastic plan for being in a relationship with His creation yet, He took on flesh and blood and walked the earth again. Not since Eden and the fall of man had God been so directly present with the people He longed to love. For three years He preached salvation. For three years the majority of His people (the Israelites) rejected Him utterly. One day Jesus cried aloud over Jerusalem saying, "How I longed to gather you under my wings as a mother hen gathers her chicks, but you would have no part of Me." Soon after, He was crucified by the very nation He came to save.

Jesus rose from the dead and ascended back to Heaven to be with His Father and to prepare a place for His people to be with Him forever. As a Jewish bridegroom would leave his fiancé and go prepare a home for her, Jesus has gone to His Father's house to prepare our eternal dwelling with Him as His bride. He longs for the day that He will be reunited with His Church.

In the meantime, He is with us still. If the time of Jesus walking on earth was the most personal interaction between God and man, the time we live in now is the most intimate. Those who belong to Jesus by faith in Him now have His Spirit literally dwelling in our bodies. He is as close to us as the air we breathe. Jesus was WITH His followers. The Spirit is IN His followers.

The final chapter of human history is yet to happen, but it has already been written. As Revelation 21 plainly tells us, God Himself will make His dwelling among His people directly again. His presence will fill heaven and earth and He will "tabernacle" (dwell) in the midst of us forever and ever. Sin and death will have been banished to Hell forever, and there will be no possibility of separation between God and Man again.

It makes sense that WE would anticipate this state of being with eagerness and longing. But can we even begin to grasp that God the Father, Son, and Spirit also anticipates this state of being with great longing?

Read John 17:24. What does Jesus desire?

The word translated "desire" in this verse means:
"to will, have in mind, intend; to desire, to wish; to love; to like to do a thing, be fond of doing; to take delight in, have pleasure"

How could we doubt God's love for us? All of human history can be summarized in the story of God's longing to share Himself with people – and people's blatant rejection of Him.

On the one hand, He is committed to His glory, so He cannot just wink at sinful humanity and be a sort of Grandfather in the sky. But on the other hand, He truly loves us. He needs nothing from us, but He has chosen to set His affection on us to such an extent that He will go to any lengths to bridge the gap between our sin and His holiness and draw us in. He does not content Himself to stay aloof and offer us heaven one day; He descends time and again to walk with us and dwell with us. He condescends to walk in a garden, live in a tent, be laid in a manger – all so He can be near us. And now, He puts His Spirit in our aging, decaying, corruptible flesh so He can be as near to us as any Person can be to another. He does this knowing that as the Israelites of old turned from the temple to idols, we will turn again and again to sinning with the very bodies He inhabits.

How, Then, Should We Live?

Read 1 Corinthians 6:20. What should we do and why should we do it?

Read Deuteronomy 6:5. What are we to do?

Now read 1 John 4:11 & 19. What are we to do, and why are we to do it?

In light of His worth, we seek to bring Him glory – to act like Him and reflect His nature. In light of His great love for us, we love Him and we love others for His sake. It is the very least we can do!

Lesson Three

The Care and Feeding of a Spiritual Life

In Lesson One, we discovered that the Christian life is not just a matter of believing the right facts (if it were, we could grow by the strength of our minds). It is also not just a matter of obeying the right rules (if it were, we could grow by the strength of our willpower). Instead, we learned that a Christian is one who has been born again – "born of the Spirit" (John 3:5-6). The nature of that new life is not flesh (merely human); it is spirit – sharing the nature of God Himself. For that reason, it requires spiritual means by which to grow.

Remember the opening illustration of the plants and pets killed by the wrong environment and the wrong kinds of food? In this lesson, we are going to see that our spiritual life requires certain conditions in order to thrive and grow.

So what does that mean? What exactly is it that we need in order to grow strong and mature in our Christian faith?

Proving the Premise: Two Kinds of Life; Two Kinds of Nourishment

First, we need to establish clearly that there are two kinds of life – physical and spiritual – and that they are sustained by two different kinds of nourishment.

Example One: Jesus' Temptation by the Devil

Read Matthew 4:1-4.
When it says that Jesus was hungry in v.2, does this mean his body was physically hungry? (Don't be afraid of the fact that the answer seems obvious – it is!)

In v.3, when Satan tempts Jesus to turn the stones into bread, does Satan mean physical bread that Jesus can eat and alleviate His physical hunger?

In v.4, Jesus answers Satan's temptation by quoting a verse from the Old Testament. Jesus says, "Man does not live bread alone (meaning physical bread that you chew and swallow), but on every word that proceeds from the mouth of God." Here Jesus implies that during the 40 days that He has been fasting (going without food) something else has been keeping Him going: the Word of God. There is much to that statement, but for now the important thing for us to notice is that Jesus is making a distinction. *There are two kinds of food: that which feeds the stomach and that which feeds the spirit.* The body is strengthened by one, and the spirit is strengthened by the other.

Example 2: Jesus' Ministry to the Woman

In a previous lesson, we read John chapter 4 where Jesus speaks to the woman at the well. Turn to John 4 again.
Read John 4:6, 7, 8.
What are we told about Jesus' physical condition in v.6?

What can we guess about Jesus' physical condition by His request in v.7?

What can we guess about Jesus' physical condition by the disciples' errand in v.8?

In the verses that follow, Jesus not only explains the gospel to the woman and brings her to faith in Him, but He also ends up teaching and speaking to a crowd of people who come out from the town to meet Him. So, He begins the chapter tired, thirsty, and hungry. He then preaches and ministers to a crowd of people.
How would you expect Him to be feeling after many hours of this?

When His disciples return in v.27, they are more than a little surprised to see what He is up to. In v.31, what are they trying to get Jesus to do?

In v.32, Jesus tells them that He has food that they know nothing about. In v.33, they wonder among themselves whether Jesus has a secret stash of snacks somewhere. In v.34, Jesus explains that He is talking about food for His spirit. Doing the will and work of God was so satisfying to Jesus' spirit, that it made His body's hunger die down for the time being. Now, this isn't to say Jesus didn't need physical food and drink. He did. There are numerous passages that tell us Jesus ate and drank and went to dinner parties and all that. But our purpose in looking at this passage is to see, once again, that there are two kinds of life, physical and spiritual. There are also two kinds of nourishment, physical and spiritual.

This minor incident of Jesus refusing physical food in favor of spiritual food is, of course, in the greater context of His whole interaction with the woman at the well where He was giving her the very same lesson. He was using her physical thirst for water to open her eyes to her spiritual thirst for a relationship with God through Him. So the entire story, from beginning to end, illustrates plainly the two kinds of life and the two kinds of nourishment.

Example 3: Jesus' Rebuke to the Crowds

Read John 6:1-12.
What miracle does Jesus perform?

In another instance where Jesus performed a similar miracle, He tells us exactly why He did it.
Read Matthew 15:32. Why did Jesus feed that crowd? What was His concern?

Bodily hunger is a legitimate part of being human. Jesus was worried about the people's physical hunger. He had been teaching them for days, and He was genuinely concerned that they had had nothing to eat.

But also part of being human is the tendency to elevate the physical above the spiritual. After eating their fill of warm, fresh bread, there was the temptation to think that Jesus was in their midst to feed their bodies. Again, Jesus makes a clear distinction between the physical life and the spiritual life, placing the priority on the spiritual.

Read John 6:26-29.
In v.26, Jesus accuses them of seeking Him out for what reason?

In v.27, Jesus mentions two kinds of food: food that _____ and food that endures to _____. Which is He encouraging them to devote themselves to acquiring?

Remember in John 4, Jesus told His disciples that His "food" was to do the will of God and finish His work? Notice Jesus is using similar terms here in 6:27-29. He tells them to *work* for bread that endures eternally – bread that will feed their spirits which live forever rather than their bodies which will die.

In v.28, the crowds ask a good question: What is this work that we must do? Jesus answers in v.29. What does Jesus tell them is the "work" that God wants from them?

Now look at 6:40, where Jesus tells them what the will of God is. God's WORK is for them to believe in Jesus Christ. What is God's WILL?

From the three examples above, it is more than clear that Jesus taught there are two kinds of life, physical and spiritual, and that these different kinds of life require different foods to sustain them. The food that sustains the body is actual bread (obviously representing all kinds of food that we eat). For Jesus, the food that sustained His spirit was basically the Word, Work, and Will of His Father. Each example also demonstrates how Jesus always thought of the spiritual reality ahead of the physical, whereas his disciples and the crowds always thought of the physical reality ahead of the spiritual. Where Jesus put the focus on His relationship to the Father, men put their focus on the fullness of their stomachs. It was hard for them to accept that there was anything more real than that.

Now that we have established the two kinds of life, we will look more closely at those things that sustain our spirits – the "food which endures to eternal life" which Jesus spoke of in John 6:27.

Jesus: The Bread of Life

John 6
Remember, the context of John 6 is the feeding of the 5,000. Jesus did a miracle that made Him, to an impoverished Jewish crowd under Roman rule, the epitome of what they could want in a King. They were thinking of becoming His followers for all the wrong reasons (v.26). The people then started asking Jesus to do more miracles for them. They mentioned how in the Old Testament God rained a kind of bread from heaven each day to feed the people. This bread was called "manna." It was the main diet of the Israelites for their 40 years of desert wandering. Jesus' multiplying of the loaves and fishes clearly reminded them of the stories of manna. They want to be fed (physically) all the time by Jesus now.

In v.32-33, Jesus makes a shocking statement to the Jews. He basically tells them that the "bread from heaven" in the old days was really a symbol of Himself! Their ancestors were sustained physically by manna, but He was now here to offer Himself as bread that would sustain them spiritually forever and ever. Jesus says, referring to Himself, "my Father gives you the **true** bread from heaven." The Greek word translated *true* in that verse means "the reality that lies behind a symbol." He is saying the manna their ancestors ate was a symbol of the true bread, which is Jesus Christ.

Isn't this the opposite of how we normally think? We, as human beings, would say the manna the Israelites ate was REAL and that the eternal life Jesus offers in Himself is "spiritual." And by "spiritual" we would tend to mean LESS REAL than physical things. This is the error Jesus is trying to unravel. He is trying to explain that though physical things do exist and they are real, they are not everlasting. He, on the other hand, IS everlasting. And once again, He is trying to explain that physical food cannot sustain their spiritual life. For that life to grow, they will need something else -- HIM.

Read 6:47-51.
Manna was physical bread. It could sustain physical life for a time, but people that ate it still grew old and died. Manna did not impart eternal life. Jesus, on the other hand, is spiritual bread. He is that which sustains spiritual life – and that kind of life lasts forever!

According to v.52, are the people getting Jesus' point or are they completely missing it?

Now take a deep breath and prepare to read one of the strangest passages in Scripture.
Read John 6:53-58.

Now, before we go on, read the reaction of those who heard Jesus.
In v.60-61, what was the general response to Jesus' words?

In v.63, Jesus makes one clarifying statement. He makes it plain that he is not speaking in PHYSICAL terms (which would have been cannibalism). He is speaking of spiritual things – spiritual eating and drinking.

Now that we know what Jesus is NOT teaching, let's understand what He meant by these shocking statements. Many pages would be required to study this passage out completely because there is so much behind these verses. But for our purposes, we are going to focus just on verse 56:
"He who eats My flesh and drinks My blood abides in Me and I in him."

Remember, Jesus said the manna (physical bread) was symbolic of Him (spiritual bread). So, to understand what Jesus is to our spiritual life, let's think for a moment about what bread is to our physical life.

Perhaps the first thing we become aware of when we eat is that our hunger pangs go away. Even before our food benefits us nutritionally, it benefits us experientially in ridding us of that gnawing growl. This aspect of Jesus' benefit to our spiritual life is the first thing He mentions when He begins to describe Himself as our bread. In John 6:35, before He tells us anything else about it, He promises to stop our hunger. Let's be honest. If our stomach is growling and someone offers us food, do we stop to ask, "Is this nutritious? Is this good for me on the cellular level?" No. We just care that it will stop the hunger. In His compassion on our human frailty, Jesus gives us this assurance first. "I will stop your hunger pangs." In other words, "I will meet the deepest needs of your heart – the needs that gnaw at you and make you miserable. I will comfort you and satisfy you in a way that brings you contentment at your very core."

On the functional level, when we eat food it goes into our stomach, gets digested, then enters our bloodstream. From there, it travels throughout our entire system and nourishes every cell. Using the nutrients we get from our food, cells repair themselves, our bodies grow, we gain energy to do work, etc. Using this picture as a model, we can see then that when we take Jesus into ourselves, He moves through every corner of our spiritual being, healing us, renewing us, strengthening us, and helping us to grow. He is nutrition and energy to our spiritual life.

In verse 56, Jesus says that by "eating and drinking" Him, we abide in Him. To better understand this, let's switch metaphors for a moment and look at John 15. This is the best passage to go to if you want to understand what it means to abide in Jesus. Plus, the metaphor is much tidier than digestion: a vine and its branches.

Read John 15:1-11.
Again, we could turn this passage into a study on its own, but we will just focus on the aspects which help us understand Jesus as our spiritual bread.
The vine metaphor is not very different from the eating and drinking one. Just as our bodies are nourished by our bloodstream, a vine is nourished by the sap which flows through every branch.

Jesus makes an obvious statement in v.5. Just as a branch cut off from the vine can't bear grapes, apart from Jesus WE can do _____.
This is the heartbeat of abiding. It is utter and total dependence. It is the acknowledgement that we must remain connected, attached, and one with Jesus or we will be as good as dead spiritually.

In John 15:7, we see we abide in Christ by having His _____ abide in us. This parallels Jesus' words to Satan in Matthew 4: "Man shall not live by bread alone but by every word that proceeds from the mouth of God." His Word is food to our spirit.

In John 15:10, what else are we to abide in?

This is essential. Love, as we saw in a previous lesson, is the core of our relationship with God in Christ. We must keep His love for us and our love for Him central to all we think about in relation to our Christian life or it will cease to be a spiritual life at all. It will become a dead religion to us. It will be reduced to facts we believe and rules that we keep.

Let's review what we have learned about Jesus, the Bread of Life:
- He satisfies the hunger of our souls.
- He nourishes the life of our spirits.
- He is absolutely necessary to us; we are utterly and completely dependent upon Him.
- He nourishes us with His Word and with His love.

Application: How do we take Him in?

Taking in Jesus through His Word

Read 1 Peter 2:2. This verse speaks of our ATTITUDE toward God's word as our food. A comparison is made in this verse between a newborn (physical) baby's longing for _____ and a (spiritual) Christian's longing for _____ _. The application is obvious: we are to love and long for and cry for and greedily suck down the Word of God at every opportunity. Our zeal and hunger for it should not diminish as we mature. And, as this verse says, it is this very "milk of the Word" that causes us to grow.

But remember, it is JESUS who is the Bread of Life. It is JESUS' life that nourishes our spiritual life. Studying and reading the Bible is just an exercise in studying and reading unless we are going to His Word to encounter Him.

Read John 5:39-40.
In this passage, Jesus addressed the religious leaders – men who spent all their time studying the Scriptures. Where did they THINK they were going to get eternal life from?

Where did Jesus say they must turn for eternal life?

The Pharisees knew their Bibles, but they did not know Christ. When they studied their Bibles, they did not grow in their spirits, because they were not spiritually alive – born again. All their Bible study just fed their pride in their knowledge. "But," Jesus said, "the very Scriptures you claim to know so well speak of Me, and yet you won't come to Me…"

When we go to the Word of God, it must be to find Jesus and "feed on Him." It must never be just to get smarter – or even wiser.

Taking in Jesus through His Spirit

We have been talking a lot about hunger. Now let's look at what Jesus says about thirst. I find thirst almost more intolerable than hunger. Hunger can make me uncomfortable, but thirst can make me panic! There is something truly desperate about the feeling of thirst.

Read John 7:37-39.
These verses should remind us of Jesus' offer to the woman at the well in John chapter 4. According to John 7:37, what must the thirsty one do?

And in v.38, what must the thirsty one do?

Turn back for a moment to John 6:35. What two things must people do to have their hunger and thirst satisfied?

John 7:38 promises living water to those who come to Jesus and believe in Him. According to v.39, what is the "living water"?

Up to this point we have been saying that Jesus is the food and drink for our spiritual life. He is the One who satisfies hunger and quenches thirst. Why then this sudden shift to the Holy Spirit? Where does He come into the picture? That is an important question to address. Many people misunderstand Who (or as some think, What) the Holy Spirit actually is. There is no need for confusion. Jesus makes it quite plain for us.

Read John 14:16-20.
Jesus is preparing His disciples for the fact that He is about to be killed. He is explaining that He will have to die, but that they should not fall apart because He will rise again. But after He rises from the dead, as 14:1-4 explains, Jesus tells them He will be returning to God the Father in Heaven. So, He is saying that He will not be with them physically much longer. Jesus then makes them a promise.

In 14:16-17, what does Jesus tell them He is going to ask the Father to do?

At the end of v.17, Jesus says that the Spirit "abides with you, and will be in you." At that moment, the Spirit of God was right with them, in the physical presence of Jesus Himself. But after Jesus went away physically, the Spirit's presence would be not WITH them but IN them.

In v.18, who does Jesus say will come to them?

In v.20, who does Jesus say will be in them?

According to these verses, the Holy Spirit is actually Jesus Himself in His spiritual rather than bodily form. Can we really draw such a conclusion from this passage? I believe so. This statement is not much different from the one Jesus makes earlier in the chapter about His relationship to the Father.

Read John 14:7-9.
Jesus says plainly if the disciples have seen HIM, they have seen the _____.

When Philip says, "Show us the Father," Jesus answers, "Have I been with you so long and you don't know Me yet, Philip?" Jesus was the physical manifestation of the Father's life and nature. The Spirit is the spiritual manifestation of Jesus' life and nature. This is as far as our understanding goes. We cannot fully grasp how God can be three distinct persons (a "Trinity"), yet still just one God. But we don't need to understand that to grasp the significance of what Jesus is promising to His followers in John 14:18, 20. Jesus is saying that when He ceases to be WITH them physically, He will come to be IN them spiritually.

So much needs to be said about the Holy Spirit. But our focus in this lesson must be limited to how we feed and care for our spiritual life. For now, it is just important to understand that Jesus gives us His own life when He gives us His Spirit. His Spirit sustains our spirit in numerous ways (which we will explore in a later lesson); but He must be permitted to do so.

Two commands

We are given two specific commands regarding the Holy Spirit within us.
1. Read 1 Thess. 5:19. What are we told not to do?_____ the Spirit
   The meaning of this word is just what you would think. Do not put out the Spirit's fire. Do not throw a wet blanket over Him. Do not silence Him when He speaks. Do not ignore Him when He prompts. Do not pretend He is not there.
2. Read Ephesians 5:18. What are we to be? _____ with the Spirit
   This means to be completely overflowing to the brim. To return to the image of the bloodstream in the body, do not put a tourniquet around some part of your life and choke off the Spirit's access. Let Him invade and permeate every cell of your being. Let Him bring Jesus' own life and nourishment to every corner of you.

So...What have we learned in this lesson?
* Just as physical life is sustained by physical food, spiritual life is sustained by spiritual food.
* Our spiritual food – that which sustains life and causes growth in our spiritual self – is Jesus
* We must abide in His word and abide in His love, drawing all our life from Him
* We take Jesus into ourselves ("eat His flesh and drink His blood") by means of the Scriptures
* We take Jesus into ourselves by means of the Spirit of God, letting Him fill us completely

Remember Jesus' words: "He who comes to Me shall not hunger; He who believes in Me shall not thirst." We need only to come to Him eagerly, believing and He will be our very life. What a promise!

Lesson Four

The One Command

Quick Review

In Lesson 1, we learned that Christians are new creations, the God-begotten children of our heavenly Father with a spiritual nature growing within.

In Lesson 2, we paused to look at why God would put His life in us. We discovered He is motivated by His commitment to His glory and the depths of His love for us. We saw that all of history can be understood in reference to God's desire to be among His people in a relationship with them.

In Lesson 3, we learned that spiritual life requires spiritual nourishment, and that Jesus Himself is our "food" and "drink." He satisfies our longings and infuses us with all we need to live and grow in our Christian life. We also saw that we take Jesus into ourselves by means of reading His Word and being filled with His Spirit.

Now that we have seen how and why the spiritual life of the Christian begins, and what sustains it, we need to look at what this life produces. What does it look like in action? In other words, considering what we ARE, now what ought we to DO?

Thou Shalt...

There is a beautiful simplicity to what God asks of His children. He gives us only one command although, like a coin, it has two sides.
Read John 15:12. What is the one command Jesus gives His disciples?

Why do I say this is a two-sided coin, if that is only one command? Look at the previous verses, John 15:9-11. The context of the command to love one another is the assumption that in order to do this, a love-bond must exist between us and Christ. It is as we abide in His love that we are able to demonstrate love to one another.

This two-sided coin of the love command is seen elsewhere in Scripture.
Read Matthew 22:37-40.
What is the greatest commandment of all?

What is the second commandment, which Jesus says is like the first?

To see how important this command is, read 1 John 4:7-8. (Remember, FIRST John is the letter near the end of your Bible, not the gospel of John.) What does verse 8 tell us about the person who does not love?

Clearly, this is a matter of life or death. So, let's take a closer look at this two-sided command.

Side One: Love God

What does love for God look like? How do we know if we are loving God?

Living out our love for God is very different from living out our love for other people. Much of our love for others (as we shall see shortly) shows up in how we relate to them when they do us wrong or disappoint us or need something from us. Since God can never sin against us, and He really doesn't need anything from us, how can we demonstrate our love for Him? We find the answer in love's opposite. More specifically, we find it in the two words God uses most often to describe the sins of His people in both the Old Testament and the New: *idolatry and adultery.*

Idolatry

Read Jeremiah 8:19. What has Israel (God's people) done?

Read Isaiah 42:8. What will God not tolerate?

In these Old Testament passages, the idols spoken of were literal. They were figures carved from wood or stone. But in 1 John 5:21, John records a warning. What is it?

It is not likely, in the greater context of 1 John, that the idols John meant were the same sort that Israel worshiped in the past; but they were just as real. They were things that would usurp God's place in the hearts of His people.

Adultery

Read Isaiah 54:5. How does God describe His relationship to His people? What is He to them?

In Jeremiah 31:32, what was God to His people?

What did His people do to Him?

This Old Testament imagery is brought into the New Testament as well. Read James 4:1-4. In verse 4, what makes a believer into an "adulteress" in God's mind?

God's Jealousy

According to Exodus 34:14, God is a _____ God.

James 4:4-5 forbids us to love the _____ on the basis that it arouses God's jealousy.

In 2 Corinthians 11:2, Paul speaks in terms of being jealous over the Christians' holiness, longing to present them to Christ as a _____ bride – His alone, undefiled by adultery.

We tend to think of jealousy as a bad thing because when we as humans practice it, it almost always has a selfish element. But there is a type of jealousy that is good and pure: the husband's demand for the exclusive love of his wife. This is the kind of jealousy God feels. If a husband were content to share the love of his wife with other men, we would say that the husband had a serious problem. In the same way, if God were content to share our love and worship with other gods, that would be a flaw in His character. As the one true God, He alone deserves our worship, so He is jealous of our worship – He wants it all for Himself. But He not only wants our exclusive worship, He wants our exclusive devotion – ALL of our love.

In James 4:4-5, we are told a believer cannot love both _____ and the _____.
In 1 John 2:15-17, what is the command?

In Matt. 6:24, what does Jesus say is impossible?

Why is it impossible?

So, how do we demonstrate our love to God? We give Him our exclusive worship and devotion. We give Him an undivided heart. We repent of our idolatry (having other loyalties that compete with Him). We repent of our adultery (having other loves besides Him). We give Him our whole heart.

Side Two: Love One Another

But, you may say, if the second great commandment is to love others, how can we give God all of our love? Where then will we get the love with which to obey the second commandment?

The answer to this question is the key to our ability to obey!

First, we must obey the first commandment. We give all of our love to God alone. We must love Him, as He demands, with ALL of our heart, ALL of our soul, ALL of our mind, and ALL of our strength. All means all. We must hold nothing back. After we have done that, God then pours His love out through us that we may obey the second command and love one another. The love with which we love others is not our own meager supply of human affection. It is the bottomless well of God's own love.

Read 1 John 4:7-11. This passage explains in detail that our love for others originates with God's love for us and ours for Him. But the core truth is found in verse 7. Where does love come from?_____

If we have any doubts about our inability to produce love on our own, we need only read Galatians 5:19-21. What kinds of actions are typical of human nature?

In Galatians 5:22-23, we have a very different list. These things are the fruit of the _____.

The fruit metaphor points us back to John 15:1-5, 8 where we began. To bring these verses to life in their application, we could insert any of the fruit of the spirit listed in Galatians 5 into this passage in the place of the phrase "bear fruit." For our purposes here, insert "love(s)" in the blanks below, then read it aloud to yourself:

"I am the true vine, and my Father is the vinedresser. Every branch in Me that does not _____, He takes away; and every branch that _____, He prunes it that it may _____ more. You are already clean because of the word I have spoken to you. Abide in Me and I in you. As the branch cannot _____ of itself, unless it abides in the vine, so neither can you (_____) unless you abide in Me. I am the vine, you are the branches; he who abides in Me, and I in him, he _____ much; for apart from Me you can do nothing.. By this is My Father glorified: that you _____ much and so prove to be My disciples."

We give all our meager love to God. He gladly accepts it as worship from His dear children. Then He transforms it, making it into His very own perfect love, then pours it back through us (Romans 5:5) into others. If the love originated in our nature, God would not be glorified by it -- WE would. Remember, God is glorified when His character is made visible. When we become channels of HIS love, He is glorified in us.

If we had to love others with only our own human love as a supply, we would run out so quickly! But in Jesus' hands, He does to our love what He did to the five loaves and three fishes (John 6). What in mere human hands could have fed only one young boy, in Christ's hands fed a multitude.

The Kindness in the Command

From a human standpoint, it seems odd to think of demanding all of a person's love for oneself. Is God being selfish to ask us to give Him our whole heart? Shouldn't He just let us love others directly? Why put Himself in the middle?

It is actually the greatest kindness for God to ask us to love Him first of all because He alone is perfectly lovable. If we would stop and think about it, we would realize that He should be the easiest of all Persons to love! By making Himself the One whom we are really loving when we love others, what could otherwise be seen as a burden becomes a delight!

Consider one final passage on this topic: 1 John 5:1-4
Notice in verse 1 the passage begins where we began in Lesson 1: being born of God. All that is expected of us hinges on the fact that we have the God-begotten spiritual life in us. At the end of v.1, what is the basis for our love for one another?

In v.2, how do we know that we have love for each other? What comes first?

In v.3, what does John say about God's commandments?

In v.4, why are the commandments not a burden to us? What has happened to us?

The passage comes full circle, beginning and ending with our God-born new nature as the basis for our ability to love God. Then our love for God becomes the basis for our loving one another.

The Content of the Command: 1 Corinthians 13:4-8

If we had to come up with REAL love all on our own, we would be at a total loss. Especially considering what love actually is...
- Love is patient
- Love is kind.
- Love is not jealous (envious)
- Love does not brag and is not arrogant
- Love does not act unbecomingly
- Love does not seek its own way
- Love is not easily provoked
- Love does not take into account a wrong suffered
- Love does not rejoice in unrighteousness but in the truth
- Love bears all things, believes all things, hopes all things, endures all things
- Love never fails

Try inserting your name in each statement below and see how you do:
- _____ is patient
- _____ is kind.
- _____ is not jealous (envious)
- _____ does not brag and is not arrogant
- _____ does not act unbecomingly
- _____ does not seek its own way
- _____ is not easily provoked
- _____ does not take into account a wrong suffered
- _____ does not rejoice in unrighteousness but in the truth
- _____ bears all things, believes all things, hopes all things, endures all things
- _____ never fails

Now insert Jesus' name in each statement above. Suddenly it seems like a pretty decent arrangement, doesn't it? This kind of love is the fruit of His Spirit. As we make Jesus the sole object of our devotion, He pours this kind of love through us into others. We become able to relate to others in this way. We find ourselves patient, kind, forgiving, and generous – truly loving in word and deed. The love is His, but the change in us is real!

Fruit-bearing and Our Union with Christ

When we talk about love, we usually have something a little more personal in mind than a vine and its branches. After all, we are people, not plants. If our love for Christ is to be like the love a branch bears for its supporting vine, that is intellectually interesting but not really emotionally satisfying.

But remember, we are made in the image of God. The affections and needs of our hearts are a reflection of what exists in His own heart.

Read Romans 7:1-6.

As with most Scripture, there are many layers to what is being taught here. But for our purposes, what is the relationship between the believer and Christ compared to?

In verse 5, Paul writes of the condition of the unbeliever trying to bear fruit (good deeds or things like love, joy, peace...) but all they can produce is what?

In verse 4, Paul speaks of our "marriage" to Christ and says that this relationship bears fruit (offspring) for God. This metaphor of marriage teaches the same truth as the vine and the branches, but it makes us realize that our bond to Christ is not an impersonal, sterile thing. It is as vital as a marriage. He is not a vine – He is a Person. His union with us is personal and individual. That union, Christ in us by His Spirit and us in Him by our faith, produces fruit for God. And the greatest of all fruit is Love.

Lesson Five

The Means, the End, and the Fruit of Abiding

"The fruit of the Spirit is love, joy, peace, patience, kindness, goodness, faithfulness, gentleness, self control…" (Galatians 5:22-23)

As we look at this list, I think we would all agree that these things are the keys to happiness in the Christian life. Love would help us in all our relationships – from the boss to the in-laws. Joy, well, who doesn't want to be joyful? Peace would help us cope with stress. Patience would make us better parents – and drivers! Kindness would help in the workplace or on that church committee. Goodness would make us feel better about ourselves. Faithfulness is certainly essential to a strong marriage. Gentleness would make us more tactful friends. And self control – just what we need for success in everything from the household budget to that pesky diet. Yes, we want this fruit and we want it now!

In this lesson, we are going to learn how to abide in the vine so this fruit is produced in our lives. But before we do that, we need to take a closer look at the title of this lesson.

The Means, the End, and the Fruit of Abiding

At first glance, this title may seem wrong. Isn't abiding the "means" and fruit the "end"? Don't we abide in order to bear fruit? If we do, we have fallen into the oldest trap in the Bible. Before we take another step toward abiding, we must have this straight.

The MEANS is abiding.
The END is our union with Jesus.
The FRUIT is love, joy, peace, etc.

Read John 17:1-3.
God sent Jesus here to give eternal life to men. What is eternal life?

Read John 17:20-26. Jesus' prayers reflect not only His own deepest desires, but the perfect will of God the Father.

What does Jesus ask for in v.21?

In v.24?

In v. 26?

We abide in Christ in order to enter into a perfect union with Him. That is the ultimate goal of our existence as Christians. Everything God does in us moves us to this greatest good: oneness with Christ. If we achieve this and nothing else, our life has been fully satisfying to God. He has accomplished the purpose for which He saved us. The fruit of the Spirit is the outcome of that union – the offspring of it, so to speak. But it is not the only reason for its existence.

Just as bearing children should never be the only reason for a couple to enter into a marriage, obtaining the fruit of the Spirit in our lives should not be the only reason we want to abide in Christ. Don't misunderstand. Just as having children is a good and right thing to do in a marriage, so also bearing fruit is a good and right outcome of abiding in Christ. But we are too self-loving at our core. We cannot trust ourselves to approach God without having this distinction clear: If we only want to abide in Christ because we want joy or peace or self control, then we are idolaters at heart. Just as we would look critically upon a woman who enters into a marriage indifferent to her husband but bent on having children for herself, we must look critically at ourselves if we want to draw near to Christ in order to get what He has that will make us into better people.

An exaggeration?

Maybe this seems like splitting hairs, a chicken and the egg argument, to you. Doesn't it all look the same in the end? Do we have to make such a big deal of motives? We bear fruit for God; God is glorified. Isn't that enough? How can seeking the fruit of the Spirit be a step toward idolatry?

Seeing God in terms of His promised gifts has been a stumbling block to God's people since day one. All the way back in Eden, Eve seemed to weigh her allegiance in the scales of fruit promised. She put the innocence and purity of walking sinlessly with God in one side of the scale and knowledge of good and evil in the other side and chose knowledge.

Israel also committed this sin. We won't take the time to re-cap their history and failures in this study. But if you were to read Deuteronomy 6-11, you would see a pretty complete summary of what God promised to them – and what He desired from them. Basically, God promised them health, prosperity, and safety if they would worship Him alone and make no alliances with the inhabitants of the land God was giving them. They were to drive out the Canaanites and leave no one behind. Then they were to establish the worship of the Lord in that land. He would dwell among them and they would worship Him. He would protect them from invasion and make sure they had rains and crops. God was essentially promising them a "happily ever after" in exchange for their devotion to Him alone.

In no time, Israel proved that their hearts were NOT set on having their God dwell in their midst. They were not excited about worshipping and serving Him alone and passing along the heritage of holiness to their children. They did not care about being a light to the nations, showing that their God was the One true God. They cared about what God promised them: prosperity and safety. These things were to be the FRUIT of their union with God. Instead, they made the "fruit" into the "end" – their goal. This made faithfulness to God secondary to obtaining prosperity and safety.

Before long, other things started to promise the same things God had promised. Making an alliance with a neighboring nation (instead of driving them out) seemed a better way to get safety than worshipping God. Enslaving the inhabitants and exploiting their labor (instead of driving them out) seemed a more effective path to prosperity than loving God with all their hearts. Before long, even making an offering to the pagan god Baal seemed a more direct way to get rain for crops than worshipping the true God.

This continued off and on for years. Even Solomon, supposedly so wise, fell into this trap. To obtain what God would have given anyway in exchange for drawing near to Him, Solomon married foreign princesses to make alliances, taxed his people into poverty to build palaces, and amassed horses from Egypt to protect his borders.

Do you see the connection? God promised Israel that certain things would come as a byproduct of their relationship with Him. They set their hearts on those things – not on God Himself. Today, God does not promise us health, wealth, and safety. He promises us the fruit of the Spirit. But if we set our hearts on the fruit, not on the relationship of abiding in Christ, we are no better than Israel. Sure, it looks nobler to pursue the fruit of the Spirit than health, wealth, and safety. But is it really nobler? If, for example, we just want God because we want self control to break our bad habits, is that less selfish than Israel's desire for peace and safety? I think not.

The Danger

In fact, if we are only seeking to abide in Christ as a means of producing this fruit, what will keep us from pursuing other means of producing it if Christ does not work fast enough for us – or if the fruit does not look like we expected it to? If we want the fruit and not the relationship, what will keep us from turning to Oprah, Dr. Phil, pop-psychology, or even pop-culture if those will give us the same outcome we are looking for? Anger management, parenting techniques, self-help, money management, diet motivation, relationship coaching – all these are available from the world. And if these are why we want the fruit, we will quickly abandon Christ. He will not deliver in a way that satisfies us, because He will not let us get away with using Him that way. He will not be mocked.

A Final Metaphor

It may seem I am belaboring this point, but that is only because it needs to be belabored. In our pragmatic age of methods and systems, the church has fallen out of love with Christ and into love with His benefits. We want what works. If Christ works, we want Him. If He doesn't we will accept a counterfeit. And the evil, deceptive heart within us says, "Why does it matter HOW I become loving, HOW I find joy, HOW I develop patience, kindness, or self control, just as long as I develop these things in myself?" To continue the metaphor we began with, that is like a wife saying to her husband, "So long as we have children, why does it matter who the father is?"

Read Galatians 3:1-5. As you read, mentally insert "human methods" for the phrase "works of the Law."
What two things (methods of Christian growth) is Paul contrasting in the passage? (see especially v.3, 5)

Read Galatians 5:25 and fill in the blanks:

"If we _____ by the _____, let us also _____ by the _____."

Remember everything we have learned so far? Our salvation is a spiritual birth. It produces a spiritual life in us that must be fed with spiritual food. That life comes through the Spirit of Christ. The food that our spirit lives on is Christ Himself. If we think we can sustain a spiritual kind of life with the ideas and methods of people who know nothing of Christ – or worse, are openly hostile to Christ – we are seriously mistaken.

There is only one kind of fruit an unbeliever's life can bear. What is that, according to Romans 7:5?

The counterfeit fruit produced in our lives if we use the world's methods may look a lot like the real thing at first. But it will not stand the test of time. Its pleasures will be short-lived (Heb.11:25); and most of all, it will not bring glory to God. Paul had such "fruit" in his life before he believed in Christ. Consider his attitude toward that "fruit" after his salvation.

Read Philippians 3:7-9. What does Paul think of his old fruit now?

What does he care about now, more than anything else?

The Means of Abiding

Now that we have established that the goal of abiding in Christ is to be one with Him in a way that will bear fruit for Him, let's look at how we go about abiding in the vine. In all of Scripture, Old Testament and New, three activities emerge again and again. These three set apart sinners from saints, idolaters from faithful ones. They are the characteristics of the abiding soul:

1. Time spent in prayer
2. Time spent in the Word of God
3. Time spent in worship

These three can be further divided in this way:
1. Time spent in Prayer
    a. Scheduled times
    b. Spontaneous, continuous time
2. Time spent in the Word of God
    a. Disciplined, structured study
    b. Continuous meditation
3. Time spent in worship
    a. Regular, corporate worship
    b. Continuous, individual worship

Let's see these practices in Scripture. We are only going to look at a small sample, but there are many more examples that could be cited.

Time in Prayer

In Daniel 6:10, what was Daniel's habit regarding prayer?

In Mark 1:35, what is Jesus' habit regarding prayer?

Isaiah 50:4 is a passage that prophesies about Jesus' life as a man. From this passage we see that it was Jesus' habit to meet with God early each morning for prayer. This is an example that we would be wise to follow. If the Son of God felt He needed this time with His Father at the start of each day, why should we think we can survive without it?

In Revelation 8:3-4, what are the prayers of the saints compared to? How are they represented figuratively in this passage?

Read Exodus 30:1-8. In this passage, God is giving instructions for how He was to be worshipped in the tabernacle – the tent where His Presence was going to dwell among His people. This tabernacle had specific pieces of furniture in it which represented actual things in Heaven. The tabernacle was sort of like a model of God's throne room in Heaven. The events you read about in Revelation 8 were actually taking place in heaven. The commands in Exodus were meant to model those heavenly realities. In Revelation 8, we saw that the incense burned on an altar before God and the fragrant smoke that went up from that incense was symbolic of the prayers of the saints.

Keeping that in mind, look at Exodus 30:7-8 again. When was Aaron (the priest) supposed to actually burn incense on the altar?

Even in His design for the tabernacle, God indicated that He wanted His people to come to Him in prayer at consistent, set times in a disciplined manner. Morning and evening prayers would be a healthy habit for any Christian serious about abiding in Christ to build into their routine.

Prayer- Continual

But saying our morning and evening prayers is certainly not enough for us to achieve an abiding life. Prayer needs to be as much a part of our spiritual life as breathing is to our physical life.

What does Paul command in 1 Thessalonians 5:17?

What does he command in Ephesians 6:18?

In Ephesians 1:15-16, what is Paul's habit?

In Colossians 1:9, what does Paul say he does?

In Romans 1:9-10, what does Paul do?

Continual or Continuous?

According to Webster's dictionary, *continual* means to do something repeatedly over an indefinite period of time; whereas, *continuous* means to do something without stopping – ever. To illustrate what this means, think of our meals. We eat continually, meaning we eat three meals a day every day. But we stop eating at the end of each meal. So our eating is not continuous. Our breathing, on the other hand, is continuous. We breathe all the time without stopping. Continual eating and continuous breathing are necessary to life.

Our prayers are to have both a continual (regular intervals of disciplined prayer) and a continuous (never stopping) dimension.

The Greek word used in Romans 1:9-10 (translated "unceasingly") is the same one used in 1 Thessalonians 5:17. It literally means "without intermission, incessantly, without ceasing." Paul is very clearly advocating and practicing a state of continuous prayer.

But on the other hand, we know Paul slept and preached and wrote letters and had conversations with friends. He could not have been talking to God at the same time he was talking to other people. So, was he simply exaggerating – or is there more to prayer than talking?

An Open Connection

In John 11:41-42, Jesus is just about to raise His friend Lazarus from the dead. He prays aloud, thanking God for hearing His prayer. Then Jesus says something like, "You always hear me, but I am saying this for the benefit of the people here so they will know that You are behind this miracle."

Jesus indicated that He had a state of silent communication going on inside Him with the Father all the time. His formal prayer out loud was just for the sake of the people hearing. It was an extension of the ongoing conversation between Himself and the Father which they knew nothing of.

In John 17:13, Jesus says something similar. Why does Jesus say He is speaking that particular prayer out loud?

Aaron in the tabernacle burned incense in the morning and the evening; but I am positive that the aroma of that incense lingered in the tabernacle all day and all night. A tent structure made of fabric with just one door and no windows would certainly have absorbed the smell of the fragrant smoke. So, God could truthfully say that though incense was burned just twice a day, the smell of it filled His nostrils perpetually. This is a picture of our prayer life. There are times of focused prayer and then there is the fragrance of prayer always about us. Both Jesus and Paul slipped in and out of conversation with God frequently as they went about their business so that they could honestly say that they "prayed without ceasing." There was never a time that they stopped praying.

Time in the Word

Again, we will look at an Old Testament example and a New Testament example, to demonstrate that time in God's Word has always characterized His devoted followers.

In Ezra 7:10, what three things had Ezra devoted himself to?

In Deuteronomy 17:18-19, what did God command that every king of Israel should do when he first came to his throne?

In 2 Timothy 2:15, what are we told God's workman must be able to do?

In Titus 1:9, what should God's servant be able to do?

In Hebrews 5:12-14, what is the writer rebuking the Christians for?

There is an expectation that those who want to abide in Christ will spend time in His Word – diligently studying it so that they can teach it to others and handle it accurately. All believers should be knowledgeable in sound doctrine, familiar with the teachings of Scripture. This only comes through disciplined, careful study.

Continuous Meditation

But just as prayer has a continual and a continuous aspect, so does our time in God's Word. We are to study continually but also to meditate continuously.

What is the command in Joshua 1:8?

Read Psalm 1:2. When does the "blessed man" meditate on Scripture?

Read Deuteronomy 6:4-9. When are we to be focused on God's Word?

Read Proverbs 6:20-23. The teachings referred to as coming from the parents in this passage are the teachings about the Law of God (as in the passage above). List several things these teachings will do for the one who binds them around their neck (keeps them in the front of their minds at all times).

Time in Worship

The subject of worship is so broad, it could be a topic of study in and of itself. Many books have been written on the subject. But for our purposes, we are going to give a simple, two-pronged definition.

Read Psalm 29:1-2. What are God's holy ones commanded to do? (The phrase is repeated several times.)

The first aspect of worship is to recognize God's incredible worth. It is to ascribe to Him all the glory that His attributes deserve. Worship involves telling God out loud all that He is – all that we know Him to be. It is holding Him up high in our minds and bowing ourselves low in His presence.

Read Psalm 50:14-15. What are we told to do in verse 14?

What does God say honors Him in verse 15?

The second aspect of worship is to recognize our desperate need. It is to see God as all-sufficient and ourselves as in constant need of His care and rescue. If you were to read from the beginning of Psalm 50, you would see that God is correcting His people for an error in their approach to Him. It seems they were viewing their sacrifices to God as something that He actually needed from them. Their worship had come to mean a time they gave things to God —as if He did not own everything already! God corrects their thinking and tells them that a worshipper must come in thankfulness and in dependence. When we call out to God for rescue, and He rescues us, that is what honors Him. John Piper once said that the best way to honor an inexhaustible fountain is not to bring a bucket of tap water to dump into it, but rather to fall on your face and drink from it gratefully and eagerly.

In a phrase, worship is raising our eyes to Christ. It is looking upon Him in His splendor. It is also looking to Him in our need. And as in Bible study and prayer, worship has both a continual and a continuous dimension to it.

Corporate Worship

In Acts 2:42-47, when the Church was just getting started, what were the habits of the people?

Read Hebrews 10:25. What are believers supposed to do consistently?

All throughout the New Testament is the assumption that God's people will gather together continually (regularly and consistently) to worship Him together. In fact, we are commanded not to neglect this kind of assembling together. But references to corporate worship are just a blip on the screen of the Bible compared to the numerous Scriptures that speak of worshipping in the private place of our own spirit. This inward worship makes up the **continuous** part of our worship.

Private Worship

Read John 4:19-24. Remember the woman we met in lesson 1? She wanted to worship God correctly, so she asked which mountain God wanted to be worshipped upon. Jesus told her instead that God was seeking _____ worshippers who would worship Him in _____ and in _____.

This worship – the adoring, seeking, dependent Godward gaze of the heart – is what God wants from His people.

Read 1 Chronicles 16:8-11. List the commands in these verses.

Notice in verse 11, the command is to "seek the Lord and His strength. Seek His face continually." This verse sums up worship beautifully. It includes both the adoration and the dependence of a true worshipper.

List the phrases that refer to the gaze of the soul upon God in the following verses:

Psalm 16:8

Psalm 25:15

Psalm 105:4

Psalm 27:8

Psalm 121:1-2

Psalm 123:1

And in the New Testament:

Hebrews 12:2. What are we to fix our eyes upon?

Colossians 3:1-2. What are we to set our minds upon?

A true worshipper is one who has his gaze fixed upon Christ day and night. A worshipper looks to God, both in adoration of His attributes and in dependence on His provision, every moment of the day. To take our gaze off of Christ is to say something else is more lovely to look at. To look somewhere else in our time of need is to say He is not enough for us. To live in a state of worship is to think about Him all the time. Every moment that our minds are not absorbed in something necessary to doing our duties as human beings, we should default to thinking about God and Christ.

This may seem impossible, but it has been the practice of devoted worshippers for thousands of years. It takes practice and mental discipline, but if we want to know God like Abraham or David or Paul knew God, we must cultivate this Godward gaze.

A Final Practice: Eagerly Await His Appearing

Something must be said, as we close this lesson, on the way the follower of Christ views His return. The teaching of Jesus on abiding (John 15) is sandwiched between two passages that speak enthusiastically about His return. We have looked at these already in a previous lesson. In John 14:1-3, Jesus compares His return to the Jewish wedding tradition. He is a bridegroom, gone to His Father's house to put on an addition in expectation of His return to claim His bride and take her home forever. We have also looked at John 17:24, where Jesus speaks to the Father of His desire for His followers to join Him where He is, in all His glory. But in the mean time, we are here "in the world but not of the world (17:16)." Our hearts are already with Christ, our treasure in His presence (Matt.6:20), our gaze fixed on Him (Heb.12:2), our minds set on things above where He is (Col.3:1).

The writers of the New Testament reflect their longing for Christ's return. Record their phrases on the subject below.

Peter- 2 Peter 3:12-14

Paul- 2 Timothy 4:8

John – Rev. 22:20

Jude- 1:24

If we are to be ready for His return, we must be diligent to abide in His Word and in His love (John 15:7, 9). We must devote ourselves to prayer (1 Peter 4:7) and be true worshippers, with our gaze fixed always on Christ. If we do these things, we will be a fruitful branch. We will find that our lives are heavy with the fruit of love, joy, peace, patience, kindness, gentleness, goodness, meekness, and self control. We will bear fruit for God – to His glory, and will enter into the joy of our Master forever (Matthew 25:21).

Remember, the MEANS is abiding. The END is joy in the Master. The FRUIT is the outcome of abiding.

Lesson Six

The Helper

In Lesson 5, we learned that there are three activities that are absolutely essential to living the Christian life: prayer, Bible study, and worship. These are the heartbeat of the abiding life. As we focus on these exercises of our union with Christ, the fruit of the Holy Spirit grows naturally in our lives like grapes on a healthy vine.

Before we move away from this topic, we should look a little more closely at the Holy Spirit. He is the sap running through the vine. He is our life-connection to Christ Himself. And He is the one who helps us to do the very things required of us to abide in Christ. We would be lost without Him – in every sense of the word!

Another Helper

In John 14:16, Jesus promises, "I will ask the Father, and He will give you another Helper, that He may be with you forever." The word *another*, in the Greek, means another one of the same kind. In other words, Jesus is sending a Helper Who is just like Himself. We saw in a previous lesson that Jesus refers to the Holy Spirit dwelling in His disciples as synonymous with He Himself dwelling in them. They are both Persons of the same God. To have the Spirit is to have Christ Himself within.

The Greek word translated *Helper* means "one who comes alongside to give aid." Some Bible translations use the word "comforter." Others use the word "advocate" or "counselor." All of those meanings are included in this word. But the most literal rendering is *Helper*.

Help in Prayer

Read Romans 8:12-30 carefully and slowly. In verses 14-16, what does the Holy Spirit testify of to our spirit? In other words, what does the Holy Spirit convince us is true, deep down in our hearts?

Read John 16:23-28. How is prayer going to change for the disciples after the Holy Spirit comes to them? What will be different about how they approach God in prayer?

Read 1 John 5:14-15. What confidence are we supposed to have in prayer?

We need to understand that we are God's beloved children in order to pray effectively because that relationship is the only basis for our approaching God in faith. The Holy Spirit gives us that confidence in prayer. But there is another reason we need the Spirit's help to pray.

In Romans 8:26-27, why do we need the Holy Spirit's help in prayer? What does He know that we don't?

In verses 28-29, we are told what God's will (or, purpose) for each one of us is. What is His purpose for our lives?

Not only does the Holy Spirit convince our spirits that we are the beloved, adopted children of God, He also helps us to pray for the right things – things that have to do with our becoming more and more like Jesus.

Read 1 Corinthians 2:10-12.
These verses point out that just as a man's spirit knows that man's thoughts, God's Spirit knows God's thoughts. How could we possibly know what goes on in the mind of God unless the Spirit of God revealed it to us? The focus of these verses is "what God has prepared for those who love Him." God's Spirit reveals to us what God has given to us in saving us (v.12). The Spirit tells us what God has done for us and what He has in store for us. The Spirit helps us to grasp the depths of our relationship with God and all that it means to us now and for eternity. So, how does that help us to pray?

Read John 14:12-14. What is the promise in verse 14?

In John 16:23, what is the promise?

In Mark 11:24, what do we have to do in order to get what we ask for from God?

To pray in Jesus' name means to pray for the very same things He would pray for. The only prayers we can pray with the kind of confidence described in Mark 11 are prayers that are definitely God's will. In order to pray God's will and pray in Jesus' name, we need to know His mind. We need to know what He wants. That is how the Holy Spirit helps us in prayer. He reveals to us the mind of Christ and then helps us to pray according to that mind. He knows the will of God and He intercedes for us, translating our feeble prayers to match that will.

This is exciting because it shows us that by the very act of praying, we come to know God better. The Spirit teaches us about the very mind of God as we pray in the Spirit. Of course, this can only happen if we are spending a good deal of time in prayer – and if we are listening to the quiet promptings of the Spirit, not just praying down a list without thinking about what we are saying.

Help in Bible Study

The second aspect of abiding in Christ is reading, studying, and meditating upon the Word of God. For this, too, we are completely dependent on the help of the Holy Spirit.

Read 1 Corinthians 2:13-16.
God's word communicates _____ truths in _____ words to _____ people.

Remember our first lesson? A natural man is born of the flesh; a spiritual man is born of the Spirit. The kind of truth that God has for us in His Word is spiritual truth. It cannot be understood simply with the natural mind. An unbelieving person without the Spirit of God within them will read the Bible and consider it foolishness. It will make little or no sense to them. And it will certainly not feed their soul. We, however, have the Holy Spirit within us. He is able to bring the Scriptures to life in a way that builds us up in the knowledge of God.

Read 2 Peter 1:20-21. How did the Scriptures come to be written? Who was behind the writing?

\

Read 2 Timothy 3:16. All Scripture is _____.

The word "inspired" literally means "God-breathed." In Scripture, the Spirit of God is associated with the "breath" of God. (John 20:22) The Bible was written as the Holy Spirit moved men to write down what He wanted them to say. So, essentially, the Bible is the Spirit's book.

In Ephesians 6:17, the Word of God is referred to as the _____.

Since there is such a deep connection of authorship between the Holy Spirit and the Word of God, it only makes sense that He would be the One to help us understand it. In the following passages, list either how the Spirit is described or what the Holy Spirit does for us:

John 14:17

John 14:25-26

John 15:26

John 16:12-15

1 John 2:20-21

1 John 2:27

The Holy Spirit is the mind of Christ in us (1 Cor. 2:16). He is the messenger of Christ sent to take all the truth of Scripture and turn the lights on in our hearts and minds so that we can see it clearly; understand it; and, by His power, obey it.

Help in Worship

The Holy Spirit's role in our ability to worship God is absolutely fundamental.
Fill in the blanks from John 4:24.

"God is _____, and those who worship Him must worship in _____ and truth."

If we were not spiritually alive, we could not worship God. As we saw in lesson one, it is the seed of the Spirit that brings forth a new kind of life in us – a spiritual life which is capable of relating to God.

The Holy Spirit also helps us to worship by placing us in the presence of God. In the Old Testament times, men worshipped God by going to the temple and offering sacrifices. Where is the temple now, according to 1 Corinthians 6:19?

According to Romans 10:6-8, how near is Christ?

Read Hebrews 10:15-22.
This passage talks about the fact that we have access to boldly enter the presence of God in both prayer and worship. According to verse 15, how do we know that we have this access to God? Who tells us this?

Another way that the Holy Spirit helps us in our worship is by making God knowable to us.

In John 4:22, what was wrong with the Samaritans' worship? What hindered them?

In Acts 17:22-23, what defect did Paul observe in the worship of the men of Athens?

In John 9:35-38, what did the man healed of his blindness need before he could worship Jesus?

In John 16:14-15, what exactly does the Holy Spirit do for us?

The Holy Spirit enables us to know God. He reveals God to us so that we do not have to build an altar to the Unknown God in our hearts. He takes what is Christ's – Christ's knowledge of the Father, His oneness with the Father, His attributes and nature and will – and communicates it to us so that we can relate to God meaningfully. We can adore Him and exalt Him and praise Him in truth because we know the truth about Him. The Spirit of truth is the One who makes that possible.

Final Thoughts on the Spirit

Read 2 Corinthians 1:22, 2 Corinthians 5:5, and Ephesians 1:14. What is the Holy Spirit called in these passages?

Read 1 John 2:20, 27. What is the word John uses for the Holy Spirit in these verses?

At first glance these terms might seem very different. What does a down payment have in common with an anointing? But upon reflection, we see that they are teaching us the same thing about what the Holy Spirit means to us.

The common link between them is found in the name Paul uses for the Holy Spirit in Ephesians 1:13: "the Spirit of _____."

As anyone who has purchased a home (or even put an item on layaway in a department store) knows, a down payment is a partial payment that guarantees that the rest of the payments will follow. By referring to the Holy Spirit as a "down payment" God is promising us two things: first, that there is more to come; and second, that what is to come is of the same kind as what we have already received.

The Holy Spirit is eternal life within us. He is ours forever, forming a connection to God that cannot be broken. Because He is God's own life in us, we know that there is more of God's life to come for us. He is a partial answer to the prayer of Jesus in John 17 that we would be one with Him and with the Father. What an engagement is to a marriage, the indwelling Spirit is to the union that is to come. It is a foretaste, yet what is to come is both more and better.

Like a down payment, an anointing is also a promise of greater things to come.

In the Old Testament two kinds of people were anointed: kings and priests. David the shepherd boy was anointed to be king by Samuel (1 Sam.16:13). At that time, Saul was the king in Israel, and his son Jonathan was next in line to the throne. The anointing was a statement of God's intention that David would rule over His people. It was a promise of things to come before it was an actual fact. David had to wait several years before the throne became his. But David knew the nature of God. For God to promise a thing was as sure as the thing itself. David never wavered in his confidence that he would rule Israel one day. He fought a giant and was endlessly pursued by his enemies, but his life was literally indestructible. He could not die until God's promise was fulfilled.

By calling the indwelling Spirit our "anointing," John is indicating two things. First, he is affirming that we are priests of the Most High God (1 Peter 2:9). We have continual access to the presence of God by virtue of the position we have in His Spirit (Heb. 4:16). Secondly, he is indicating that one day we will reign with Him in glory (2 Tim.2:12). We have great things in Christ now; but there are greater things yet to come. The Holy Spirit is our guarantee of all that eternal life in God has in store for us.

"But it is written, 'What no eye has seen and no ear has heard, and what has never come into a man's heart, is what God has prepared for those who love Him.'

Now God has revealed them to us by the Spirit, for the Spirit searches everything, even the deep things of God."

1 Corinthians 2:9-10 HCSB

Lesson Seven

Clean Hands; Clean Feet
Confession and the Practice of Christian Fellowship

The Christian church has been around for over 2,000 years. In that time, certain words have been overused, redefined, and stripped of almost all their original meaning. Every once in awhile, someone has to go back and recapture that lost word and put the meaning it originally had back into it or the Church will lose something precious.

One word that has lost its meaning in recent days is worship. Most churches today have what they call "Worship Teams." These are basically song leaders. If you go to a Christian bookstore today, the "worship" section will be made up of music CDs. In our current usage, when we say "worship" we tend to mean singing. This was not the case centuries – or even several decades – ago. Worship certainly includes singing songs of praise and adoration to God, but it is also much more than that. We talked about worship in lessons 5 and 6. We saw that worship is the Godward gaze of the spirit. It is looking to God and adoring Him for His attributes, fixing our hearts and minds on Him, loving Him, ascribing to Him the worth that is due Him. It is also bowing before Him in our neediness and dependence, having a correct sense of our own proportion in relation to Him. And it is the presentation of our entire life in devoted service to Him, leaving all idols behind. Worship is an exclusive devotion to God alone. It is a tone set throughout our entire being. It is understanding that we are set apart for Him and Him alone. When we only think of worship in terms of singing songs of praise to God, we lose a huge element of what the Spirit-born Christian life is meant to be.

A second word that has lost its meaning is fellowship. We have degraded this word even more than the other. The church I grew up in had a room called Fellowship Hall. This was a large tiled room adjacent to the kitchen where church dinners took place. Every Sunday morning, pastors all over America say something like, "Join us in the lobby after the service for a time of fellowship." By this, they mean coffee, doughnuts, and chit chat. Many churches hold "Fellowship Dinners" on a regular basis. All of these activities are good and create an atmosphere of friendliness and warmth, but if we reduce our understanding of fellowship to eating together, we have lost something vital in the life of the believer. Just as worship is so much more than singing, fellowship is so much more than eating.

Fellowship Identified

Many passages allude to fellowship, but in 1 John chapter 1, we have the very core of fellowship laid out for us in a clear context. Read all of 1 John 1, then go back through the chapter and answer the following.

In verse 3, who has fellowship with whom?

In verses 6 and 7, what is necessary in order for a believer to have fellowship with God?

What is necessary in order for a believer to have fellowship with other believers?

Read 2 Corinthians 6:14-15. What is necessary in order for two people to have fellowship?

Fellowship Defined

In the Corinthian passage above, we saw that in order for a Christian to have fellowship with another person, that person must also be a Christian. In the First John passage, we saw that the other person must not only be a Christian, but an obedient Christian. Two people walking down a street together must either both be walking in darkness or both be walking in the light. One can't be in the dark and the other in the light. That is the basic message of 1 John 1. The reason becomes clear when we consider the definition of fellowship.

The Greek word for fellowship used in these passages is *koinonia*. The root of this word means "an association, a companion, partner, participant." The word implies partaking or sharing together due to a common interest. There is an assumption that two people in fellowship share a common set of beliefs, priorities, and goals. They are pulling in the same direction. They want the same things. They have a fundamental bond between them that connects them in spite of how different they may be in personality or background.

Fellowship Illustrated

Consider Jesus' disciples. Included among the twelve were Matthew and Simon (not Simon Peter, but another Simon). Matthew was a Jewish tax collector. This was not just like working for the IRS in our day. Matthew was considered a traitor by the Jews because he collected taxes for Rome from the Jewish people. Rome was the conquering empire. Matthew worked for the "enemy." Simon, on the other hand, was a zealot. That means before he left all to follow Jesus, he had worked (perhaps violently) to get the Romans out of Jerusalem. He was a political agitator. So, how could a traitor and a zealous patriot live and eat together side by side for three years? What bond could possibly be strong enough for them to call each other "brother"? Jesus! When they chose to follow Jesus, all other loyalties and causes fell away. Following Jesus, learning from Him, and spreading His gospel became the center of their lives. They could have fellowship with one another because they shared this essential thing in common.

Fellowship Explained

On the human level, we can understand fellowship fairly easily. There is a level of fellowship shared even by sports fans and movie-goers. People bond around common interests all the time. But Christian fellowship is much different from typical human fellowship – or at least it should be. Unfortunately, often our idea of fellowship does not rise much above that level. Just as people who see each other at the same gym several times a week might develop a sort of camaraderie, those of us who see each other at church each week feel an affinity for one another. But that is not biblical fellowship.

Christian fellowship must start with God. Just as Matthew and Simon had to form a bond with Jesus before they could form one with one another, we must have fellowship with God before we can have true fellowship with one another.

Fellowship with God

Read 1 John 1:3 again. You will notice that John is saying that he has fellowship with God. The reason he is eager to have fellowship with the believers to whom he is writing is that he wants them to also share in fellowship with God. Then John's fellowship with them will be a fruit of their fellowship with God.

How on earth can human beings have fellowship with God? Let's begin by thinking of what that means, exactly. According to our definition, to have fellowship with someone means that you are in a partnership with them, participating together in something, and seeking the same goal. It implies a unity of desires and activities which puts you constantly shoulder to shoulder with the other person. Can a man claim to have this with God?

Read 1 Corinthians 1:9. Can we have fellowship with God?

From this verse, how do you know?

Read 2 Corinthians 13:13. With whom do we have fellowship?

Clearly from these Scriptures we see that it is God's intention that we have fellowship with Him. But what would we call this fellowship? Consider the progression in the verses below.

In John 13:13-16, what terms would apply to the Christian's relationship to Christ?

In John 15:15, what term does Jesus use for His followers?

What makes the difference between a slave and a friend? What does the Master do differently with a friend?

In John 20:17, what term does Jesus use for His followers?

The fellowship that is offered to us as Jesus' followers is not just the common bond of a slave and his master – where the slave is committed to the good of the master's estate because he depends on it for his own room and board. The bond is not just that of one friend to another, where one takes some interest in the other's affairs, but he has affairs of his own to tend to as well. The fellowship bond between us and God is that of an adopted child and a Father. God's interests are our interests because we are family. His gain is our gain. His loss is our loss. His kingdom is our kingdom. His home is our home.

Fellowship with One Another

In the passages above, we see that Jesus refers to His disciples as His brothers only after his death and resurrection. This privileged position was purchased for us by the cross. This gracious act on God's part demands a response on our part.

Read Philippians 2:1-4. In light of the fellowship we have in the Spirit of God, what does God want us to do? (List several things.)

Read Romans 12:4-5. What is our relationship with one another compared to?

In Ephesians 4:25, how is our relationship to other believers described?

Much could be said about our relationship to one another as the "Body of Christ." That is a topic for another time. For now, just realize God intends for us to consider one another's good to be our good. That is what it means to be in fellowship with each other.

Fellowship Maintained

Clean Hands

When we place our trust in Jesus alone for our salvation, we become "born again." As we learned way back in lesson 1, we become spiritually alive. That act can never be reversed because the very nature of the life we receive from God is eternal life. It never dies and never ends because it is God's own life – His own Spirit. But there is something we can lose in our relationship with God: fellowship. Remember, in order for us to have fellowship with God, we need to be walking with Him in the light. He will not walk with us in darkness. If we choose to walk in darkness (sin) then we lose our fellowship with God. We do not have Him as our companion and partner. We are alienated from Him like a disobedient son or daughter.

Turn back to 1 John 1:5-10. In verse 7, when we come into the light, what happens to our sin?

In verse 9, we are told how we come back into the light. What must we do?

If you have any Catholicism in your background, perhaps the word "confess" makes you think of going into a little booth and telling a priest everything you have done wrong. This is another word that has lost some of its meaning to us today. Confessing is more than just listing our sins. And since confessing our sins is how we get them washed clean, it is important that we understand exactly what confessing means.

One of the best ways to understand a concept is to look at its opposite. In v.10, what is the opposite of confessing our sins?

Read John 3:19-20. Jesus is using light and darkness in this passage in much the same way that John uses it in his letter. What kind of people love darkness?

Why don't they want to walk in the light?

Turn to Ephesians 5:1-13. Read the entire passage, then answer these questions:
What kinds of deeds do people try to hide under the cover of darkness?

According to v.8-10, what does it mean to walk in the light?

Verse 13 emphasizes again that the way to get rid of sin is to drag it into the light and expose it. This is confession. It is taking things we have done that we would like to hide or deny and dragging them into the light and admitting, yes, this is what we have done. When we pull our secret sins out into God's light, we have to admit not only what we did but how our deeds look in the pure light of day. What looks like frugality in the dark can be shown for greed in the light. What looks like admiration in the dark can be shown for lust in the light. What looks like anger in the dark is shown to be a murderous heart in the light. What looks like a bad habit in the dark is shown to be an idol in the light.

First John 1:8 is very clear. If we deny that we have sinned, we are deceiving ourselves. We have broken fellowship and we are walking in the darkness. But, verse 9 is a bright ray of hope. If we confess our sins, God is faithful and just to forgive us our sins. This does not only mean He is faithful, in the sense that we can count on Him to do it. It means that because of the shed blood of Christ God's faithful and just (fair and righteous) nature demands that He forgive our sins. Not only does He forgive in the sense of covering over the stain of our sin, but He forgives to the extent of washing that stain away and making us completely clean again – inside and out.

Read James 4:8. What analogy does James use for confessing our sins? What act does he compare it to?

This analogy is helpful because it is so much a part of our lives. No matter how clean we are from our morning shower, our hands need washing numerous times throughout the day. In fact, we are now being told by various medical associations that hand washing is our number one line of defense against all kinds of viruses and illnesses. Our bodies may be clean, but our hands need washing all the time or we are in danger of contaminating ourselves and others.

Confession is meant to be practiced very much like hand washing. Unlike the Catholic tradition of only confessing when you are in a church in the presence of a priest, James tells us to draw near to God ourselves and wash our hands immediately so we can enjoy fellowship (nearness) with God again right away. The moment we are conscious of something sticky on our fingers, don't we rush to wash them? In the same way, the moment we are conscious that we have done or thought or said something that is a sin against God (not pleasing to Him) we should pause immediately and confess that. Drag it into the light. Point to it. Admit it by name. Then forget it, knowing that it is washed away by the blood of Christ and it is no longer an obstacle to fellowship with God.

Read Psalm 32:5.
What did David, the writer, do?

What did he NOT do?

What did God do?

This is the model for confession. Cleanse your hands, sinners, and draw near to God! He will forgive completely and draw near to you again. Fellowship need not be lost for more than a moment.

Clean Feet

When our hands get dirty, we can see the dirt immediately. It is easy enough to wash them and move on. Many (perhaps most) of our sins are ones we are immediately aware of. If we are sensitive to the conviction of the Holy Spirit within us – that little nudge in our spirit that says, "You should not have done that!" – we can keep our hands fairly clean on our own.

But in our Christian walk, there are times we really need one another to help us in this struggle to stay free from sin. I want to suggest to you that one of the most neglected aspects of Christian fellowship is this: washing one another's' feet.

Turn to John 13:1-17 and read the entire passage before answering the questions below.

Jesus does something to the disciples here that he then commands them to do to one another (v.14-15). What is it?

I am going to concede right from the start that it is possible that Jesus is speaking of physical realities here. It is possible that He intends for His disciples to physically wash each other's feet as an act of humility and loving service.

However, I would like to suggest that even if He did intend it to be practiced physically, He also intended for it to be practiced spiritually. There may be a physical application to Jesus' command to wash one another's feet; but I do not believe that the *only* application of this command is physical.

Take the command in the larger context of the book of John. When Jesus offered the woman at the well living water, was it physical water or spiritual? When Jesus said that His followers were to eat His flesh and drink His blood, was the application of that teaching to be physical or spiritual? John is a book of metaphors, imagery, and word pictures. Some we have touched on in this study (such as water, bread, and vine) and others we have not (such as Jesus being the good Shepherd and the door). In a book filled with pictorial lessons, I believe this is yet another picture.

So, if it is a picture, what is it a picture of? What does Jesus intend for us to do for one another that foot washing symbolized?

In John 13:6, how does Peter feel about Jesus washing his feet?

In verse 8, Jesus tells Peter if He does not wash Peter, Peter has no part in Him. Would that make sense if Jesus was ONLY talking about having clean feet?

In verse 9, Peter then asks Jesus to wash his hands and head as well – in other words, give him an entire shower if that is what it takes to have his part in Jesus. What does Jesus tell Peter in verse 10?

For clarification on what Jesus meant, turn to John 15:3. In this verse Jesus says the disciples are already
_____ because of the _____ He has spoken to them.

In both John 13 and 15, Jesus is teaching that faith in His Word (the gospel) is what gives a person a clean heart. Salvation or new birth is a state of cleanness before God. When we sin, we pick up dirt on our hands and feet, so to speak, but our heart is still clean before God. That condition is never altered by our actions.

Read Hebrews 10:19-22.
In verse 22, our hearts are clean because they are sprinkled with what? (see v.19)

Our bodies are washed with what?

This verse makes the interesting distinction between the once-for-all cleansing of our hearts by the blood of Jesus and the ongoing cleansing of our bodies by water, which allows us to approach God boldly in prayer.

So what does this have to do with fellowship and foot washing?

Just as hand washing is how we rid ourselves of our conscious sins, I believe foot washing represents the application of the cleansing word of God to one another's lives in a way that helps us see and overcome the sins we may not be aware of.

Read James 5:16. What is commanded?

Now read verses 19-20. What role can we have in a fellow Christian's life, according to this passage?

Read Galatians 6:1-2. What are we to do for one another?

Read Matthew 7:3-5. Once we have cleared away the sin in our own life, what ought we to do for our brothers and sisters in Christ?

I began this section by saying that this aspect of fellowship is the most neglected in the church today. How common is it for believers to confess their sins to one another? Not nearly as common as pot luck dinners, I would guess. How common is it for one believer to come alongside another and point out the areas of sin they have observed, with the goal of helping that believer back into the light, so fellowship with God can be restored fully? How open are we to having our blind spots pointed out to us? Are we willing to let other Christians help us clean those hard-to-reach places so we can be free from sin and approach God with a clear conscience? Or are we like Peter, refusing to have our feet washed?

Fellowship Modeled

Look at Hebrews 10 again. We saw in verse 22 there was a reference to being washed with pure water. Read the very next verses (23-25). In the immediate context of talking about being washed clean, the writer gives a command in verse 24. What is it?

And then in verse 25, what are we not to forsake? What are we to do frequently and consistently?

Why are we to assemble together? What is the purpose?

In the New Testament context, people did not assemble just to hang out with other Christians. They met to spur each other on to love and good works, to encourage each other to stay pure and unspotted by the world. They met to confess their sins and pray together so they could have fellowship with God and with one another. Acts 2:42 tells us that the very first church's Christians met continually, devoting themselves to "the apostles' teaching and to fellowship, to the breaking of bread, and to prayer." Now that we understand better what that means, we can follow their example and try to recapture some of what has been lost from the practice of the word "*fellowship*."

Conclusion

Why should we care about having clean hands and clean feet? Because that is what is required in order for us to have fellowship with God. If we lose our fellowship with God, we are not much better off than an unbeliever. We will not have the love, joy, peace, patience, etc. in our lives that God intends for us to have. Sin will grow up like weeds and form a barrier between us and God so that we will not be able to approach Him in prayer or worship.

Jesus paid a very high price for us to be able to be reconciled to God the Father. But He did not pay it grudgingly. He paid it eagerly! In Hebrews 12:1-2, it says that "for the joy set before Him" Jesus endured the cross. What was that joy? We see it in John 20:17, after He rose from the dead. He sees Mary and tells her to go back and give the disciples this message: "I ascend to My Father and your Father, My God and your God." You can't miss the tone of exuberance and joy in His words. Jesus is delighted to usher us into the same relationship He has with His Father. He means for us to share that intimacy – that fellowship. That is what He died to accomplish. He does not simply intend for us to populate Heaven one day in the future. He intends for us to know and walk with Him now – today!

In 1 John 3:1, John writes, "See how great a love the Father has bestowed on us, that we should be called the children of God!" We are meant to enjoy that relationship, not in name only but in experience every day. But that can only happen if we approach God with a clean heart, clean hands, and clean feet. God provides the clean heart, but we must wash our hands and feet ourselves. In the Old Testament, the priests had to wash their hands and feet in a basin called the laver before entering the temple to worship God. What they did physically, we must do spiritually.

God does not demand that we be sinless in order to approach Him and walk with Him. He only demands that we bring our sin into the light and admit it. The one thing God will not tolerate is us hiding our sin.

Read Psalm 32:1-5.
What happened to David when he tried to hide his sin?

What happened when he confessed it?

Denying our sin, excusing it, explaining it, hiding it, rationalizing it – all of these God cannot and will not tolerate. All of these are a form of lying to Him and, as 1 John 1:10 says, calling Him a liar. When God's hand of conviction was heavy on David, making him feel miserable about his hidden sin, if David had said, "I have not sinned," he would have been calling God's Spirit a liar for pointing out a sin to him that was not real. Do we understand how serious this is? To contradict the Spirit of God when He convicts us of sin is to actually call God Himself a liar! How much better it would be to simply come into the light, admit to our sin openly and honestly, and then receive forgiveness and begin to walk hand in hand with God again.

In Matthew 18:21-22, Peter asks Jesus, "If my brother sins against me, how often do I have to forgive him? Seven times?" Jesus answered, "Not seven, but seventy times seven." That was His way of saying forgive until you lose count – then keep forgiving! If God expects us to forgive in this way, would He Himself do any less? When we confess our sins, forgiveness is certain; and fellowship is fully restored.

Lesson Eight

Our Blessed Hope:
Living IN this World, but FOR the Next

If you read books and articles written by the earliest church fathers , from the New Testament writers through several hundred years after Christ lived on earth, you will see a common theme: eager anticipation of Christ's return. The hope of an eternal dwelling with God one day sustained even the Old Testament saints, like Abraham. Hebrews 11:10 tells us that Abraham's great faith came from the fact that he was "looking for the city which has foundations whose architect and builder is God." He was content to live in tents on earth, moving from place to place with no permanent home, because his real hope was fixed in Heaven, where God dwelt.

In the Gospels, Jesus tells numerous stories that have a single moral: Live as faithful servants whose master could return at any moment. We are to constantly expect Jesus' return. Knowing that He could show up at any time is meant to motivate us to serve Him faithfully while we wait for Him.

Consider these stories. Write down what each passage teaches us about being ready for the Lord's return.

Matthew 24:42-51

Matthew 25:14-30

Luke 12:35-38

Luke 12:42-43

The passages above emphasize the dread of not being faithful to the Lord at His return. But Jesus also emphasized the positive aspects of His return.

Our Hope

In John 14:1-3, what does Jesus tell us will happen when He returns?

Now turn to First John 3:1-3. In verse 2, what will happen to each one of us at the moment that we come face to face with Jesus?

In verse 3, what does John tell us we should do in response to this hope?

When Jesus returns, we shall be transformed instantly into our sinless state. We shall be "like Him," John says. That process of becoming like Christ has already begun, but it will be perfected when we see Him. Paul refers to this transformation as well.

Read 2 Corinthians 3:18.
When you look in your bathroom mirror, whose image do you see?

Notice in this verse, when we look in the mirror, we do not see ourselves, but we see the glory of Christ. And as we gaze upon Him, we are transformed to match that image. As we behold Christ, fixing our eyes on Him, we become more and more like Him each day. One day, when we finally meet Him in person, the transformation will be complete.

This is also the imagery evoked in Hebrews 12:1-2.
What is the Christian life compared to in these verses?

Where are we to fix our eyes?

Notice Jesus is referred to as the "author" and the "finisher" of our faith. This Greek word means, "one who makes a beginning; the author or source of anything." Jesus is the one who sets our spiritual life in motion. He is the starting line, the source, for our eternal life. But He does not just wind us up and let us go. He is also the "finisher" of our faith. This Greek word means, "a completer, perfecter, one who reaches a goal so as to win the prize." Jesus puts our life in motion and then sees it through to a guaranteed finish.

What is the promise in Philippians 1:6?

When will the "perfecting" take place?

The "day of Jesus Christ" refers to the day that Jesus returns for us. Paul is saying exactly the same thing as John: When we see Jesus, His work in us will be perfected. We shall be like Him.

This way of understanding Jesus as "author and finisher" is so important that it appears in numerous passages, including the book of Revelation. In Revelation, Jesus reveals Himself as the glorified King, the ruler of Heaven and Earth. He is so magnificent that John falls down before Him like a dead man when he sees Him. In this book, Jesus calls Himself by many different names that describe the full extent of His authority and power.

In Revelation 1:8, what name does Jesus use for Himself?

The *alpha* is the first letter of the Greek alphabet, and the *omega* is the last letter. This is another way for Jesus to emphasize that He is the author and perfecter, the beginning and the end. He is the One who begins things and the One who guarantees their completion.

In light of Jesus' role as Alpha and Omega, read John 10:27-30. Read these verses carefully, fully absorbing what they promise you. According to Jesus' words, is it possible that you can begin your spiritual life and not complete it? Can Jesus fail to bring you to the "finish line"?

Our Response

Returning to 1 John 3:3, we see that our response to this hope of being like Christ one day is to purify ourselves. On the one hand, it is Christ who brings us to perfection, but on the other hand we are not to be passive. We are to actively purify ourselves.

But what does it mean to "purify ourselves"? We can't wash ourselves clean from our sins. Only Christ can do that. So, what is God asking of us? The Greek word used here means to sanctify or to set apart. We are meant to set ourselves apart for God. This word is similar to the one used in Romans 12:1, where Paul says that we are to "present our bodies as a living sacrifice, *holy* and acceptable to God." In this passage the idea is also to give ourselves to God. We are to offer our actual bodies to Him, dedicating our existence to His service. We are to see ourselves as belonging to Him – which, in fact, we do!

What does 1 Corinthians 6:20 tell us about our bodies?

Turn to 1 Peter 1:14-19. The word translated "holy" in this passage is the same root word as used in 1 John 3:3.

What is the command in v.16?

How are we to live, in v.17?

What were we bought (or "redeemed") with, in v.18-19?

The Means and the End – Again

In this study we keep coming back to the reasons for what we do. And the reasons always center in our union with God in Christ. The goal of holiness and purity is not just to be holy and pure. The goal is to be able to dwell in God's presence and be at home there.

To get a picture of what is required to be in God's presence, read Exodus 19:20-25. What would happen to the people if they came up to the mountain where God's presence was dwelling?

Now Read Leviticus 16:1-14. This passage describes how Aaron, the High Priest, was to approach the Ark of the Covenant. This was the golden box in the tabernacle where God's presence was located during the time of the Israelites' travels in the wilderness. God Himself dwelt in the Holy of Holies between the golden cherubim on the Ark of the Covenant.

What would happen to Aaron if he did not follow all the washing and sacrifice rituals in approaching the presence of God?

God is a consuming fire (Hebrews 12:29). He is completely pure and free of all contamination. He cannot allow Himself to be in the presence of sin. The most graphic illustration of this is seen when Jesus was on the cross.

In Matthew 27:45-46, what happened while Jesus was on the cross?
Read 2 Corinthians 5:21. What happened to Jesus on the cross that would explain why the Father had to forsake Him, or turn His back on Him, there?

We can never be at home in God's presence while we bear the stain of our sin. Yet, we are destined to live in His presence forever. Therefore, we must be purged from all our sin. It should be our aim in this lifetime to move as close to Christ's likeness as we possibly can. That is how we honor Christ's sacrifice. It is how we show God that being with Him and being like Him is the goal of our existence. As John put it, if the hope of our life is to be like Him, we will begin to purify ourselves even now.

How We Purify Ourselves

First John 5:18-21 are John's last exhortations in this letter. They are the summary statement of what he considers most important for the readers to retain and put into practice. He makes three statements that begin with "We know…" By affirming what we know, we learn how to purify ourselves in expectation of Christ's return.

Purity in our Spirit-Born Nature

The first affirmation John makes is this: "We know that no one who is born of God sins; but He who was born of God keeps him, and the evil one does not touch him." (5:18)

This reminds us of what we learned in lesson one of this study. We have a nature within us that is conceived of the Holy Spirit and born of God Himself. This "new man" does not sin. Whenever we do sin, we have chosen to act out of our old, fallen nature. We have reverted to a way of being that is supposed to be dead and gone. Sin should be an abnormal occasional deviation for us, not the normal state of our existence. By remembering we have a nature born of God that does not sin, and focusing our minds on that, we can avoid walking in sin. According to this verse, it is Jesus who keeps us and prevents the evil one (Satan) from getting his way with us.

Purity in Relating to the World

Verse 19 tells us that we are of God, and the whole world is of Satan. The world is our enemy. The idea behind "world" in this context is not individual people being our enemy. It is the whole system of thought that leaves God completely out of the picture. It is the system that is hostile to God and denies Him at every turn. Separately, as individuals the world is made up of people God loves and people for whom Christ died. But as a collective whole, the world is against Christ and will be against us. That is what John meant when he said the whole world "lies in the evil one."

Read John 17:14-17.
In v.14, how will the world feel about us Christians?

In v. 15, what does Jesus ask God to do?

In v.16, Jesus compares our relationship with the world to His own. In verse 18, Jesus compares our mission in the world with His own. As the Father sent Him into the world, so He sends us.

What does Jesus pray in v.17?

The word *sanctify* carries the same meaning with it as "purify" in 1 John 3. Our relationship to the world can be described in that one word. To be sanctified means to be set apart for God in our hearts while geographically being located in this world.

Read 1 John 2:15-17.
According to v.15, if we love the world can we also love God?

Verse 16 lists three things that are characteristics of the world. What does the world value?

The world can seem like a formidable enemy. Christians can be made to feel foolish for believing that God created the world. We can be made to feel like outsiders for not entering into the world's pleasures. We can be made to feel like failures for not prioritizing social status or financial success. But John gives us the final word on the world in 1 John 5:4-5. In the conflict between the followers of Christ and the world, who is ultimately going to come out victorious?

What is the victory that has overcome the world?

Purity in the Knowledge of God

First John 5:20 tells us the third thing that we know: we know God! Jesus has given us understanding that we may be able to know God. The same God who is unapproachable in His holiness, whom the Israelites feared to look upon, who is a consuming fire who set the mountain ablaze with His presence, this same God is knowable to us!

Remember in John 14:8, Philip asked Jesus to show them the Father? In verses 9-10, what was Jesus' answer to him?

Jesus came to give us eternal life. According to John 17:3, what is eternal life?

Our eternal life begins the moment we come to believe in Christ. The Spirit-born life is an indestructible, eternal kind of life. This is a holy life. It is a life that continues forever in Heaven, but which we can begin to live now today. If we are to purify ourselves now in preparation for Heaven later, we must come to see our life in Christ now as one continuous thing with our life in Heaven forever. Remember, we learned the Holy Spirit is a down payment – a partial giving of the whole to come. We are in God's presence now, truly though imperfectly, because He indwells us. We should conduct ourselves in holiness during our stay on earth – just as we will forever in Heaven. (2 Cor. 7:1) We want to become in part now what we will be perfectly then. (1 Cor. 13:12)

John's Final Plea: *"Little Children, guard yourselves from idols!"*

How could John end his letter with any other exhortation? He has shown us that we must love God with all our hearts, love others out of our love for God, and abstain from loving the world. From beginning to end John shows us that our hearts must belong to God alone. Anything less cannot even be called true Christianity. Sin is idolatry. Faithlessness is idolatry. Love of the world is idolatry. Therefore, you must keep yourselves from any love that competes with your love for God.

Our great hope is that Jesus will come again for us, to receive us to Himself that we may be with Him forever. If that is the focal point of all our hopes and dreams, then we will purify ourselves in anticipation and preparation for that union. Remember our timeline of human history that we looked at in lesson 2? We saw that God has always desired to be near His people. He has chosen to set His love upon us. His plan for the ages culminates in what He describes as nothing less than a Wedding – our wedding to Christ, the Bridegroom.

Consider these words from Revelation 19:7-9.
> "Let us rejoice and be glad and give the glory to Him, for the marriage of the Lamb has come and His bride has made herself ready." It was given to her to clothe herself in fine linen, bright and clean; for the fine linen is the righteous acts of the saints. Then he said to me, "Write, 'Blessed are those who are invited to the marriage supper of the Lamb '" And he said to me, "These are true words of God."

And again, consider Revelation 21:1-7. This is the hope of which John speaks when he writes, "He who has this hope purifies himself, just as He is pure."

> Then I saw a new heaven and a new earth; for the first heaven and the first earth passed away, and there is no longer any sea.
> And I saw the holy city, New Jerusalem, coming down out of heaven from God, made ready as a bride adorned for her husband.
> And I heard a loud voice from the throne, saying, "Behold, the tabernacle of God is among men, and He will dwell among them, and they shall be His people, and God Himself will be among them, and He will wipe away every tear from their eyes; and there will no longer be any death; there will no longer be any mourning, or crying, or pain; the first things have passed away."

And He who sits on the throne said, "Behold, I am making all things new "And He said, "Write, for these words are faithful and true."

Then He said to me, "It is done; I am the Alpha and the Omega, the beginning and the end I will give to the one who thirsts from the spring of the water of life without cost.

"He who overcomes will inherit these things, and I will be his God and he will be My son.

After looking so closely at John's writings in the Gospel of John and the letter of First John, it seems fitting to conclude this study with the last words that John ever wrote in Revelation 22:20-21.

He who testifies to these things says, "Yes, I am coming quickly!"

Amen. Come, Lord Jesus.

The grace of the Lord Jesus be with all. Amen.

For Meditation and Review

Use this page for prayerful review of key principles learned in this study.

Lesson 1: The Nature of the Spirit-born Life
Word Picture: Seeds, soil, plants, and babies

- My Christian life is spiritual in nature. It begins when the seed of the Word of God takes root in my heart by faith. When God's Spirit enters my heart, a New Person is created – an eternal living being in relationship with God the Father.

Lesson 2: Created for His Glory; Saved for His Love
Word Picture: The Tabernacle – God with us!

- God created me to bring Him glory by reflecting His nature, and He saved me so I could walk with Him in love. He wants to dwell with me forever.

Lesson 3: Care & Feeding of the Spiritual Life
Word Picture: Bread and Water

- Spiritual life needs spiritual food. The word of Jesus is my bread. His Spirit is my water. He nourishes me to make me grow. He satisfies my hunger and thirst.

Lesson 4: The One Command (LOVE)
Word Picture: Vine and Branches

- God requires me to love Him and love others. This love is a fruit of His Spirit. I can only love as I abide in Him – the vine. The very love He requires of me comes from Him. When I first love Him, He then pours His love through me to others.

Lesson 5: The Means, End, and Fruit of Abiding
Word Picture: A Clock- no other way but time with God!

- I should seek God for Himself – not just His fruit. Fruit is a byproduct of relationship, not the sole reason for the relationship. Abiding requires:
  Time in Prayer- scheduled & spontaneous
  Time in the Word of God- scheduled & spontaneous
  Time in Worship- scheduled & spontaneous

Lesson 6: The Helper
Word Picture: a down payment & an anointing

- The Holy Spirit is the real presence of God in my life now with the promise of more to come. He is the first portion of my inheritance – eternal life with God forever! He helps me to pray, to understand Scripture, and to worship God.

Lesson 7: Clean Hands, Clean Feet:
Confession and the Practice of Christian Fellowship
Word Picture: Wash YOUR hands & EACH OTHER's feet

- Fellowship with God is based on walking in the light. I must confess my sins – drag them into the light and admit them. I also have a duty to apply God's Word to others' lives. This is true fellowship.

Lesson 8: Our Blessed Hope
Word Picture: the Mirror

- Jesus is the author and finisher of my faith. When I see Him, I shall be like Him! For this reason, I purify myself from all idolatrous loves, setting myself apart for Him alone.

Part Two

Keeping Right

Living the Spirit-Born Life

Introduction

In *Right From the Start*, we learned that Christianity is an entirely new kind of life. It is not just a matter of believing a set of doctrines or keeping a list of rules. It is the creation of a new life within us that is spiritual in nature. It is a life that requires spiritual food and drink to sustain it. We learned that our Spirit-born inner man is literally nourished by the life of Christ Himself. His Word is our bread. His Spirit is our water. As we take in Jesus by means of Bible study, prayer, and worship we draw life from Christ and bear fruit for God.

Right From the Start was a study about the essence of our new life in Christ and the nature of our relationship with Him. *Keeping Right* is going to be a study about putting our feet to the pavement and living that out each day. We are going to learn that our spiritual life is a reality, not a theory. It is to be practiced, not just embraced. Our Christianity is to be our defining characteristic, shaping who we are and influencing everything we do. Spirituality is not an area of our life; it IS our life. We are going to see that in the practical thoughts and actions of day-to-day life, Spirit-born people should be radically different from natural-born people. We should not think, speak, act, or process our circumstances in the same way that those without the Spirit do.

This follow-up study, *Keeping Right*, is going to be based in the book of Titus. Titus is a little book full of "big pictures." You might remember in our previous study we learned about the mirror of transformation (2 Cor. 3:18). We learned that as we gaze upon Christ the way one gazes in a mirror, our own image will grow to match His likeness. In Titus, Paul describes exactly what those reflections should look like. He tells us just what a young man or an older man, a young woman or an older woman, a boss, an employee, a citizen, or a leader should see when they look into that mirror and see Christ in themselves.

As you begin this study, do not separate it in your mind from the material that came before. This is a life, remember, not a creed or a law. We do not grow by acquiring knowledge or by exerting will power. We grow by eating and drinking Christ. What you are about to study must be taken in the context of your all-important connection to Christ as the vine. Only as you continue to abide in Him can you ever hope to grow and be fruitful for Him. Continue to review and pray over the lessons in *Right From the Start*. We will allude to them frequently. This study is another level built on that same foundation. It is not a new building that can stand on its own.

One final note: We learned in our previous study that three things are necessary in order to nurture our spiritual life: the Word of God, Prayer, and Worship. We learned that the Spirit of God operates in us through the Bible (which He inspired) and through prayer (in which He intercedes for us). We must not separate Bible study from prayer. As you do this study, cultivate the habit of praying about what you learn. You will notice that each lesson ends with a segment entitled, ***"Matters for Prayer."*** This feature is included to help you get started in the practice of praying alongside your study.

Lesson One

Titus: A Little Book of Big Pictures

The book of Titus is full of lists. It can be broken up neatly into about six little pieces, each containing a package of instructions for living the Christian life in whatever gender, role, or age bracket you find yourself in. In fact, in my experience, I have seen Titus dealt out like a deck of cards again and again. Here is the "church leader" card; here is the "older man" card, the "younger man" card, the "older woman" card, the "younger woman" card, etc. In my opinion, the way we tend to approach Titus is a classic example of losing the forest for the trees. We are so focused on each individual tree that we don't understand the full scope of the forest we are meant to be living in.

We are going to do something different. We are going to stand back and view Titus as one whole letter, just as Paul wrote it. We are going to see the lists not in isolation but in their context. We are going to get a handle on the big picture of what a Christian is meant to be.

The only way to begin is to read the book of Titus from start to finish. It is only three chapters long – less than two pages in my Bible. So, stop and do that right now.

------------------- **Do not cross this line until you have read the book of Titus!!** -------------------

The chapters in the book of Titus are like three interlocking circles. Each chapter contains three elements: a statement of the gospel, a list of positive characteristics, and a list of negative characteristics. The structure of the book emphasizes the fact that the gospel, when received into the heart by faith, produces an entirely different kind of person. In Titus, Paul sets up a vivid contrast between the ways believers and unbelievers act. He also makes it clear that the differences are not just superficial; they are fundamental. So, let's begin our overview of the book of Titus.

Big Picture #1: The Gospel

Read Titus 1:1-3.
According to verse 1, what does the knowledge of the truth lead to?

What is our hope?

Now read Titus 2:11-14.
What does God's grace teach us to do (v.11-12)?

According to v.14, what did Jesus redeem us to be?

In v.13, what is our hope?

Chapter 3 contains the longest and most thorough description of our salvation. Read v.4-8 carefully. Regardless of the circumstances of how and when we came to know Christ, these verses are our testimony. This is what God did for each of us.

In v.4, what motivated God in saving us?

In v.5, what did God do for us in saving us? How did He enact our salvation?

According to v.6, what did He pour out on us abundantly?

What is our hope (v.7)?

What are those who have believed God supposed to do (v.8)?

Big Picture #2: Godly Character

Read the following passages and list the good qualities mentioned. If qualities are repeated, you don't need to write them twice.

Titus 1:6-9

Titus 2:1-12

Titus 3:1-2

Big Picture #3: Ungodly Character

Read the following passages and list the negative character traits mentioned.

Titus 1:10-16

Titus 2:12

Titus 3:3, 9-11

Three Kinds of People

A close reading of Titus reveals a harsh reality. We would like to say that there are only two kinds of people in the world: believers and unbelievers. We would like to say that all believers are godly and all unbelievers are ungodly. But the fact is, that is not so. Paul acknowledges that not all believers behave as they should.

In our previous study, we saw that God wants His people to bear fruit for Him. He wants to grow the fruit of the Spirit in our lives as we abide in Him (the Vine). He also wants us to bring others to the knowledge of Him by how we live and speak. We see this same teaching in Titus.

Read Titus 2:14. What kind of people is God making for Himself?

In Titus 3:8, what are those who have believed in God supposed to do?

In 3:14, what are God's people to be devoted to?

There can be no doubt that God expects Christians to be characterized by their goodness – both in character and in deeds. We will look more closely at these "good works" in a later lesson, but for now we just need to understand that the result of our salvation should be a conspicuous kind of goodness that permeates all we do. If that goodness is absent, the consequences are severe.

Consequence #1- Disqualified for Work

Read Titus 1:16.
What do these people profess?

How do these people live?

When believers claim to have faith in God, yet deny Him by the way they behave, they have rendered themselves useless to God. They have failed to accomplish the purpose for which God saved them (Eph. 2:10). This verse doesn't pull any punches. Such a person is described as "detestable, disobedient, and disqualified (or, worthless) for any good work."

Of course there is always hope. Even if we have sinned so as to disqualify ourselves permanently for certain roles of formal ministry, we can still repent and return to a place of usefulness to God. Scripture encourages us with many examples of such people. David is the first that comes to mind. David committed the sins of adultery and murder. The consequences of his sin were unavoidable (the death of his child with Bathsheba); yet God, in His mercy, did not write David off forever. David continued to glorify God, both in His role as king and in the Psalms that he wrote after his repentance. In the New Testament, we see men like Peter who denied Christ, yet was later forgiven and restored. In Acts, Mark was a missionary companion of Paul's who wearied of the life of sacrifice and abandoned his ministry, yet later he returned to serve God wholeheartedly again. God's grace is always there for the repentant. But, I would guess that any of the men named above would rather they had not dishonored the Lord in the first place with their sin.

Consequence #2- Discrediting to the Message

Even worse than what disobedient believers do to themselves is what they do to the gospel message as a whole.

Read Titus 2:1-8.
At the end of v.5, what reason does Paul give for why the women should live in such a godly manner?

At the end of v.8, what reason does Paul give for being beyond reproach (having a good reputation)?

The word that is translated "maligned" (or "dishonored") in v.5 is the Greek word *blasphemeo*, from which we get our English word *blaspheme*. This word means, "to vilify; to defame, rail on, revile, speak evil." It also carries the idea of speaking with scornful insolence. When a Christian does not behave in a good and righteous way, the entire gospel message comes under attack by all who observe it. The gospel gets mocked and treated with scornful contempt. The outside world gets an opportunity to say, "See? It's all a lie. That person is worse than I am! Christianity is a farce."

Now read 2:9-10. What is the effect of a slave (or, a worker) who is diligent and honest? What does such a person do to the message of the gospel?

This word "adorn" is the Greek word *kosmeo*. It is the same root from which we get our word *cosmetics*. It means, "to arrange, to ornament, to embellish with honor, to gain honor." In other words, it means to make something look really good. When, as Christians, we behave the way God intended us to behave, our lives make the gospel look appealing. People are drawn to the unique brand of goodness that they see in us. When we are obedient, our lives speak volumes about the truth of our message and the power of God to transform a life.

In our previous study, we learned that God created us for His glory. We also learned that we bring God glory by reflecting His character – by displaying His likeness in our lives.

Read Matthew 5:16.
What happens when men see our good works?

We have now completed our overview of the book of Titus. We will return to Titus later to study it in more detail, but for now let's review what we have learned:

1. God has saved us. He has done this by shedding the blood of Jesus, His Son, and pouring out His Spirit on us to wash us and make us new.
2. When God saved us, it was His intention that we become a particular kind of person – a new kind of person, characterized by goodness.
3. When a Christian is disobedient to God (claiming to believe, yet denying Him by how they live) that Christian disqualifies himself for any usefulness to God whatsoever.
4. A disobedient Christian dishonors the gospel, giving the watching world a reason to mock the content of the gospel message and the Savior Himself.
5. An obedient Christian adorns the gospel, making it appealing and lending it credibility so that unbelievers can't honestly find anything bad to say about us or our God. This accurate reflection of God's character in our lives brings God glory.

Matters for Prayer

Take some time to pray over these things. Ask God to show you through His Spirit and His Word whether or not you are a person devoted to good works, adorning the gospel message with your life.

Remember our "clean hands and clean feet" lesson in the previous study? This would be a good time to wash your hands by confessing to God any ways that you may have maligned the word of God by your actions. It may also be helpful to let another believer "wash your feet" by giving you insight into any area that you may be unaware of in your life in which you may be discrediting the gospel.

Lesson Two

The Kingdom of God: An Alternate Reality

Up to this point, we have been speaking of our salvation in terms of the new birth. We have focused on the metaphors of the baby and the plant. Now we need to add another layer to our understanding of what happened when we were born of God. Not only did we change from a state of spiritual death to spiritual life, but we also changed citizenship or allegiance from one kingdom to another.

Read Colossians 1:13.
What did God rescue us from?

What did He transfer us into?

The Bible plainly teaches that there are two kingdoms co-existing on earth right now. There is the kingdom of darkness (the "world"), made up of those who do not know or love God; and there is the kingdom of light, made up of all those who have been made new in Christ Jesus. The kingdom of darkness is ruled directly by God's enemy, Satan. The kingdom of light is ruled by Jesus Himself. These two kingdoms grow side by side, mixing together like wheat and weeds in a farmer's field (Matthew 13:24-25) or like sheep and goats sharing the same pen (Matthew 25:32). Citizens of these two kingdoms live literally next door to each other in every neighborhood on earth, but they are as different as day and night – or at least they should be.

The Kingdom of the World

Volumes have been written on the kingdoms of God and this world. We are not going to delve deeply into these topics in this study. We are just going to focus on the basic principles that are vital to our understanding of how we are to live as distinct people of God while located in the midst of this world.

The kingdom of this world is marked by three distinct characteristics.
Read 1 John 2:16 and list the three things that are "of the world" below.
1.

2.

3.

These three things have characterized the kingdom of the world since it began. So, let's go back to the day that Satan broke ground in establishing his kingdom.

Read Genesis 3:1-6.

In v.6, list the three observations Eve made about the fruit God had told her not to eat.

1.

2.

3.

These three statements correspond directly to the ones in 1 John. First, Eve saw that the tree was good for food. This is the lust of the flesh. She could see that the fruit would be pleasurable to her senses to eat. It would taste good. ***The first characteristic of the world's kingdom is that it is ruled by sensual pleasure.*** The unashamed slogan of this world is "If it feels good, do it!" Second, Eve noted that the fruit was a delight to the eyes. It was pleasant to look at. ***The second characteristic of this world's kingdom is that it judges by outward appearances***. This perspective runs deeply in the cultures of our world. It shows up in everything from the worship of physical beauty to racism. It even shows up in the philosophies of education and behavioral psychology that care more about a person's actions than his motivations. Finally, Eve noted that the fruit was desirable to make her wise. This is the boastful pride of life. ***The third characteristic of the kingdom of the world is a desire to exalt one's self, even at the expense of others.*** Citizens of this world's kingdom are committed to themselves first and foremost. Usually this shows up in the drive to accumulate wealth, fame, and power.

Thousands of years after his conversation with Eve, Satan encountered Jesus in the wilderness and attempted to lure Him into the kingdom of darkness. Interestingly, Satan's temptation toolbox had not grown in all that time. He pulled out the same three temptations.

Read Matthew 4:1-10.

What three acts does Satan try to get Jesus to perform?

1.

2.

3.

Can you see the similarities? First, Satan tries to entice Jesus to do something to satisfy His physical flesh. Second, Satan tries to get Jesus to do an action that would be spectacular to the eyes but would spring from an evil motivation – to test God. Third, Satan tries to get Jesus to gain power for Himself by paying homage to Satan. This would have been the ultimate short cut to Jesus' acquiring dominion over the kingdoms of the world (definitely an easier route than the cross), but Jesus overcomes each temptation decisively. Unlike Eve, who called the Word of God into question, Jesus wields the God's Word like a sword and defeats Satan easily.

The Kingdom of God

It should not be surprising to discover that the kingdom of God is fundamentally opposed to the kingdom of the world.

Read Luke 16:15. Copy the second half of the verse below.

In the context of this passage, the Pharisees (religious leaders) were scoffing at Jesus' teaching because Jesus was presenting money as unimportant, and they loved money and all that it represented. So, the value system Jesus was teaching was one that they scorned. Jesus then turned around and said to them that the very things that they highly esteemed, God detested.

This upside down value system can be most clearly seen in the passage known as the "Sermon on the Mount." In these chapters (Matthew 5-7 & Luke 6), Jesus paints a full-color portrait of the citizen of the kingdom of God.
Read Matthew 5:1-12.
Remember, the first priority of the world's kingdom is physical comfort and pleasure. What does this passage imply about the value of physical comfort and pleasure in God's kingdom?

The second priority of the world's kingdom is judging by outward appearances. Read Matthew 6:1-6 & 16-18. According to these passages, should God's kingdom people do things for the sake of outward show, to look good to others?

What is their motivation supposed to be?

The third priority of this world's kingdom is the accumulation of fame, wealth, and power.
Read Matthew 6:25-34.
How does God's kingdom person view the accumulation of wealth and property?

Read Matthew 7:1-5 & 12.
How does God's kingdom person treat others?

Now, to see the contrast between the two kingdoms even more clearly outlined, turn to Luke 6:20-26. Fill in the chart below with the four contrasts in the passage.

Blessed...	Woe...
v.20	v.24
v.21	v.25

v.21	v.25
v.22	v.26

The kingdom of the world loves pleasure, wealth, power, and comfort. It sees the best possible life to be one of laughter and ease. It is populated by people who are motivated by pride and self love. It operates by means of force and control and manipulation. It sets all its hopes (and fears) squarely in this lifetime. It is characterized by a love of money and an obsession with outward appearances.

The kingdom of God is completely different. God's people are meant to be like flashlights in a dark room in contrast to unbelievers around us. Are we?

- Do we think it is a happy state to be in if we are poor and have just our daily needs and no extras? (Or are we just as obsessed as our neighbors with improving our standard of living?)
- Are we happy when we hunger because physical dissatisfaction reminds us of how deeply satisfied we are with God? (Or do we just want a burger and fries?)
- Are we content to have sorrow and cause for tears now because we know we shall be laughing with joy for eternity? (Or do we insist on being made happy somehow?)
- Are we OK with being alone and friendless on the job or in our schools or neighborhoods because we have shared our faith and people think we are stupid? (Or do we care so much about fitting in that no one knows we are Christians?)
- If we do have plenty of money, do we view that as a disadvantage spiritually – a reason for extra careful vigilance over our hearts so we don't fall into idolatry? (Or are we proud of what we have?)
- If we are full of good things now, do we seek to share all our excess so that we don't become "fat"? (Or do we hoard it up so we will be sure never to know a day's want?)
- If we are happy, do we look for ways to get in touch with the sufferings of others? (Or are we just glad we don't have serious problems?)
- If we have lots of friends and a good reputation, do we use that as a platform for sharing the gospel? (Or do we just enjoy our popularity and take care not to jeopardize it?)

Responding to the Word

Read James 1:22-25.
What is the Word of God compared to in this passage?

When we look into the Word and see ourselves for who we really are, what are we supposed to do?

In the next lesson, we are going to see that the basis for our transformation into a kingdom-of-God citizen is directly connected to our relationship to the King Himself.

Be encouraged today by these words of Jesus:

"Do not be afraid, little flock, for your Father has chosen gladly to give you the kingdom."
Luke 12:32

Remember, it is God who has transferred us into the kingdom of His Son; it is His work to make us fit to live in it!

Matters for Prayer

Spend some time looking at the lists and charts in this lesson. Don't focus on each detail. Instead focus on the "big picture" of the kingdom people we have studied. Which kingdom's citizens do you resemble most closely? Confess your condition to God. Talk to Him about the areas in which you resemble the world. Ask Him to work in you from the inside out, making you fit more and more into the pattern of His kingdom.

Lesson Three

A Family Likeness: God, Our Father

In Lesson Two we looked at the Christian life in terms of our citizenship in God's Kingdom. We learned that in God's kingdom the value system is the exact opposite of the world's. The world values sensual pleasure, outward appearances, and individual pride. God's kingdom accepts suffering in exchange for a higher purpose – God's glory. His kingdom focuses its gaze on things that are spiritual and eternal rather than material and temporal. And, finally, God's kingdom is concerned with the approval of God, not the praise of man.

In this lesson and the next, we are going to look at the Christian life in terms of our membership in God's family. In our previous study, we learned that we are "born of God" (1 John 5:1). As believers, we have an entirely new nature.

According to Ephesians 4:24, whose likeness do we bear?

Let's find out how we go about exhibiting our "family likeness" as children of God.

Imitators of God

Ephesians 5:1-2 says, "Therefore, be imitators of God, as beloved children; and walk in love just as Christ also loved you, and gave Himself up for us…"

The Greek root word behind the English word translated "imitate" is to *mimic*. To mimic means to copy exactly what someone else is doing. Those of us who are parents can probably relate to the way a small child will imitate a father or mother. Years ago when my daughter Moriah was just about three, she would occasionally come with me to the women's Bible study I was teaching. She would position a little chair in the front of the classroom next to mine. As I taught, I could see her in my peripheral vision, gesturing with her hands and moving her mouth as if she were the one teaching the class. It was slightly distracting to see my own movements mirrored so accurately; but on the other hand, it touched my heart. I just loved the thought of her, twenty or thirty years down the road, teaching a Bible study herself.

This is the way we are commanded to relate to God. As a child will copy the actions of a parent whom they love, we are to copy the character and actions of our heavenly Father.

What God Is Like

The idea of imitating God seems like the height of presumption. If we were not commanded specifically to do so, it would seem like the worst kind of sacrilege even to try. But since we have the command, we must assume that God really does expect us to become like Him in some finite way. So, what exactly is it about God that we are meant to imitate? Or, put more simply, what is God like?

God is Holy

Read 1 Peter 1:14-17.
What does Peter call us in verse 14?

According to v.15-16, why should Christians be holy?

What term is used to describe our relationship to God in v.17?

According to v.17, how are we to live?

This passage is astonishing, really. If there is one characteristic of God's that we might feel certain we could never share, it is His holiness. Yet, notice how plain the command is: Be holy yourselves. Verse 14 is similar to Ephesians 5:1 in that it connects our striving for holiness directly to our relationship to God as His children. Verse 17 reiterates that it is because we call God our Father that we must live holy lives during our stay on earth. But what exactly is holiness? Is it even possible for a human being to obey this command?

Defining the Term

The word translated "holy" in the Greek is *hagios*. The word has tremendous depth and layers of meaning in the ways it is used in Scripture. But to keep it simple, holiness has three basic aspects:
* Purity
* Consecration
* Worth of Veneration

Obviously the third aspect of holiness belongs to God alone, but the other two are part of our calling as children of our Father.

Purity

To be pure is to be free from sin. It is to be clean. We learned in our previous study in 1 John that the Spirit-born person has God's seed in him. He should not habitually practice sin. Sin should be an occasional aberration – not a norm. This is what it means to be pure.

Read 1 Thess. 3:11 - 4:8.
What term for God is used in 3:11?

What does God intend us to be like, according to 3:13? (see also Ephesians 1:4)

What is God's will for us in 4:3-4?

According to 4:7, what has God NOT called us to?

What HAS God called us to? (see also Col. 1:10)

In our previous study, we saw that all sin is both idolatry and adultery. To live an impure life is to be unfaithful to God. It is a serious matter. So, how do we become pure? If it were left to us to purify ourselves, we would have cause for despair. But with God, every command is a promise of what He intends to do for us. He does not command us to be pure in order to mock our weakness. He commands it in order for us to see His power at work.

Read Ephesians 5:25-32.
In this passage, the virgin bride is held up as the highest expression of purity. In this passage, who is the Bride?

Who is in charge of preparing the Bride, making her perfect for her wedding day?

List all the things Jesus does for His bride. (v.25, 26, 27, 29)

What words/phrases are used to describe the bride in v.26, 27?

God's purity goes much deeper than ours possibly can because God is untouched by sin. However, as we actively seek to imitate the purity of God, we will find ourselves turning our backs on things that are tainted with the dirt of sin. We will find ourselves drawn toward things that are true, honorable, right, pure, lovely, of good reputation, excellent, and praiseworthy (Philippians 4:8). These are the things the Father loves; and as we imitate Him we will grow to love them too.

God's kind of purity is an inside-out purity, not an outside-in purity. It's important for us to understand the difference because human nature is inclined toward the outside-in approach.

Read Matthew 23:25-28.
In v.25-26, Jesus compares the Pharisees to a _____.
What are they doing wrong in their attempt to be clean or pure?
This is a very practical illustration that Jesus is using. Years ago I used to have a space above my kitchen cabinets where I would display decorative dishes. Among these was a collection of coffee mugs. When I dusted these (rarely, I admit), I would only dust the outsides because that is all that showed. I had no intention of drinking out of them, so the insides didn't matter. They were just for decoration. Over time, the insides became so grimy with greasy kitchen-dust that I couldn't have gotten them clean if I wanted to. I eventually threw them away. This is the idea Jesus has in mind when He looks at the Pharisees.

In v.27, Jesus compares them to a _____.
What are they like on the outside?

What are they like on the inside?

In v.28, Jesus sums up their problem. Outwardly they appear righteous, but inwardly they are full of the filth of hypocrisy.

Outside-in purity can produce that same hypocrisy in us. This does not mean that the outward signs of purity (such as modesty, morality, discretion, standards in television viewing and music) are not important. They are very important. In Matthew 23:23, Jesus doesn't tell the Pharisees not to bother with their external observances of the details of the Law. Rather, He tells them that they should continue to observe such things but without neglecting the "weightier provisions" of the Law such as justice, mercy, and faithfulness. God does not want us to construct a Christian standard around our lifestyle yet have no heart for Him or for others. Purity begins with a heart that wants to know God and be like Him. Such a heart then produces a visible character that is chaste, modest, discreet, and careful about matters of lifestyle. We will look more closely at this topic in a future lesson, but for now just realize that purity is like a cup. In the process of scrubbing the inside, the outside gets cleaned as well; but the opposite is not true. Simply wiping the outside of the dish does not make it fit to drink from.

Consecration

To understand this second characteristic of God which we are to imitate, we will look at the Hebrew rather than the Greek word for *holy*. In the Hebrew, the word is *quodesh*. This word means, "apartness, separateness, sacredness, set-apartness." Clearly this is a characteristic of God Himself. He is entirely separate from His creation in that He is "other" than us in His very essence. He is pure Spirit, whereas we are a mixture of spirit and flesh. But what does God mean when He asks us to imitate Him in this quality of "otherness"?

Read 2 Corinthians 6:14-18.
This passage begins (v.14) with an allusion to fellowship. In our previous study, we learned that true fellowship can only exist between two believers. Two people cannot walk in fellowship if one is in the dark and the other in the light. In verse 15, we see that a believer and unbeliever cannot have fellowship with one another because they belong to two different kingdoms. The verse states that they cannot have "harmony" or agreement. The clear implication is that the believer is expected to be very different from the unbeliever in such basic ways that they are largely incompatible. As we learned in Lesson Two, the value systems, priorities, goals, etc. of the believer and unbeliever are exactly the opposite – or, at least they should be.

In v.16, what does God say He will do with His people?

In v. 17, what does God command His people to do?

In v.18, what is God's promise?

Verse 18 reveals to us God's heart. It is His desire to be a Father to us. He wants us to be His children. He wants to dwell among us and to be our God. But because He is holy, He cannot have fellowship with us the way He longs to unless we will come out to Him. He will not join us in darkness. We must come to His light.

This passage is not a call to geographical separation from unbelievers. We are not to isolate ourselves or remove ourselves from the company of those who do not know God. In John 17:15-16, Jesus prays for His followers not to be taken out of the world, but to remain in the world yet not of it – just as He was. The command in 2 Cor. 6:17 is a call to a mindset. It is not about location but about loyalty. We are to be completely set apart for God, ever conscious of the fact that we belong to Him, even while we go about our day to day lives in this world. We are to be willing to be different from those around us, content not to fit in. We are to identify ourselves with the family of God, bearing our Father's likeness unashamedly everywhere we go.

Don't miss the fact that this passage ends with God "owning" us as His children (v.18). If He is not ashamed to call us sons and daughters, how can we be ashamed to call Him our Father?

God is Gracious and Compassionate

Moses once asked God for a favor. In Exodus 33:18, Moses asked God to show him His glory. Moses had heard God's voice. He had stood before God while God was hidden in a fire or a cloud. But this wasn't enough for Moses. He wanted to see what God was really like. God explained to Moses that Moses could not survive a face-to-face encounter with Him; but He would do the next best thing. God would put Moses in a little cave and pass by him. While passing by, God said that He would pronounce His own name for Moses to hear (Ex.33:19-23).

In Exodus 34:5-7, God states His name in Moses' hearing. In the Hebrew culture, names were more than just labels. They were descriptions of the character of the one named. God cannot just call Himself Jehovah, or Yahweh ("the existing one"). This would be too much of an understatement. God adds some details to more fully flesh out who He is and what He is like. If anyone ever asks you what God is like, this is what you should say:

"The Lord, the Lord God, compassionate and gracious, slow to anger, and abounding in lovingkindness and truth." (Ex.34:6)

If these are the characteristics God chooses to identify Himself by, surely they are characteristics He would have us to emulate as His dearly loved children.

Entire books have been written on the attributes of God. A comprehensive study would be far beyond the scope of this lesson. For our purposes, we are going to focus primarily on how we as weak, finite human beings can imitate God in these areas.

Gracious

To be gracious basically means to treat other people better than they deserve to be treated. God's graciousness towards us knows no bounds. He gave us physical life, spiritual life, and His Spirit within. He gave us His Word and every blessing we enjoy from His creation. We are meant to imitate God's gracious methods in relating to people.

Read Matthew 5:43-48.
According to this passage, how does God treat His enemies? What does He do for them?

How are we to treat our enemies?

In verse 48, the basis for our loving our enemies and doing good to them is clear: that is exactly what our Father does! Do we ever stop to think about how much God does for people who either hate Him openly or deny His existence altogether? He sustains their lives. He allows them to enjoy the beauty of the earth; the pleasurable sights, sounds, tastes, and experiences of life; the wonder of intelligence, creativity, invention, and learning; the joys of marriage and child rearing; the security of financial success or political power; and countless other things. All this God gives to His enemies! Jesus makes it plain that God is our model for how we are to treat people who mistreat us and insult us. If we are to be children of our heavenly Father, we must not just tolerate them. We must actively seek to do them good.

In Luke 6:32-38, we find a similar passage.
In verse 35, what three things are we supposed to do for our enemies?

What does this verse say about God?

In Luke 6:36, what is the basis for our showing mercy to others?

Compassionate

To be compassionate literally means to share the same passions. It is more than just pitying someone in their distress. It is entering into their suffering with them. We are called to imitate God's compassion and extend it to others.

Read 2 Corinthians 1:2-7.
Notice the passage begins with a reference to God as our Father. This is central to how we understand what is to come next.
How does Paul describe God in v.3?

According to v.4, who comforts us?

What are we to do for others?

Verses 5-7 describe a cycle. God entered into our sufferings when He sent Jesus, His own Son, into this world to suffer alongside an impoverished humanity. As Jesus experienced the pains of human life, God experienced those things as well. He shared our sorrows so that He could comfort us in those sorrows (we will study this more closely in Lesson 4). Now He allows us to suffer so that we can enter into the sorrows of others. When we suffer, we experience God's comfort. We can then offer that comfort to others in their time of sorrow. It is a cycle of receiving from God and ministering to others that began with God Himself and is continued by us, as we act in His place.

Slow to Anger

Exodus 34:7 states that God "forgives iniquity, transgression, and sin" and extends His lovingkindness to a thousand generations of descendants of those who love Him. Yes, God must punish sin; but the passage places far greater emphasis on His forgiveness. Like our heavenly Father, we are to be people characterized by readiness to forgive and forget.

A Story

Read Matthew 18:21-35.
It is important to realize that the debt owed by the first servant was the equivalent of $10 million dollars in silver in today's economy. The debt owed by the second was 100 days' wages.
In light of that fact, do you think the first servant could ever have repaid his debt?

What about the second? Given a few years, do you think he could have repaid his debt?

In this parable, the king represents God and the servants represent us. The point of the narrative is that any amount of sin that a person could possibly have committed against us is nothing compared to the amount of sin we have committed against God. He has forgiven us more than we will ever be called upon to forgive anyone else. Verse 33 makes it clear what God expects from us: "Should you not also have had mercy on your fellow slave, even as I had mercy on you?"

Read Ephesians 4:32.
Who are we imitating when we show kindness and forgiveness to others?

Our willingness to forgive is not just a matter between us and God. When we extend this kind of forgiveness to others, it gets their attention. Holding grudges and withholding forgiveness is so natural to us on the human level, that when we release people from their debt to us, they cannot help but see God at work in our lives. We are showing them accurately what God's nature is like. On the other hand, if we refuse to forgive, and, like the wicked servant, throttle our fellow man for their offenses against us, imprisoning them in our bitterness, we misrepresent the nature of God. The actions of a child reflect on the Father, for good or for evil. If we Christians cannot be gracious and forgiving toward others, it makes the gospel look like a lie. We who have been released from the debt of our sins so completely should be quick to release others from their debt to us. This servant cared more about getting what was due him than about spreading the good news of his master's generosity. *Are we guilty of the same? Do we care more about our small ideas of fairness than about spreading the news of God's forgiveness?*

Another Story

Read Luke 15:11-32.
What did the younger son ask his father for?

What did he do with what he received?

What did he know about his father that made him dare to come home?

What did his father do when the son came home?

Jesus told this story to illustrate what God our Father is like. God's forgiveness is complete, instantaneous, extravagant, and restorative. How did the older brother feel about his younger brother coming home?

How did the older brother feel about his father's reception of the younger brother?

The older brother in this story is much like the first servant in the other. The older brother does not seem to be aware of the fact that he is enjoying the benefits of his father's generosity and love every day of his life (see v.31). He simply resents seeing his father lavish these on his brother, whom he clearly deems less worthy of honor than himself. He has not learned to imitate his father's graciousness. His example serves as a warning to us. We do not want to be like him; we want to be like the father – gracious, compassionate, slow to anger, and abounding in love.

Conclusion

Infinitely more could be said about imitating God, but I think we have enough here to get started. We have learned that:
- We are to copy the deeds and character of God our Father because we are His children and we love Him
- We are to imitate God's holiness by being pure and being consecrated to God
- We are to imitate God's graciousness by treating people better than they deserve, being extravagantly generous even to our enemies
- We are to imitate God's compassion by entering into the sufferings of others and bringing them God's comfort
- We are to imitate God's slowness to anger by extending forgiveness readily to all who have wronged us, knowing that we would owe God a far greater debt if He had not forgiven us our sins

This would be a daunting undertaking if it weren't for the promises of God. Consider Peter's words: "… seeing that His divine power has granted us everything we need for life and godliness, through the true knowledge of Him who called us by His own glory and excellence. For by these He has granted to us His precious and magnificent promises, so that by them you may become partakers of the divine nature, having escaped the corruption that is in the world by lust." (2 Peter 1:3-4)

Hold fast and draw near to Christ through His Word. He will do the work in you. He will make you a "partaker of His nature" – an imitator of God!

Matters for Prayer

Use the conclusion above as an outline for confessing any areas where you have not been like your Father in Heaven. Ask Him to show you if there is anyone you need to forgive as He has forgiven you. Ask God to show you His nature more clearly as you read His Word daily so that you can get to know Him better and imitate Him more fully.

Lesson Four

A Family Likeness: Christ, Our Brother

In Lesson Three, we learned that God wants us to imitate Him in the same way that little children imitate their parents. We saw that when God showed Himself to Moses, He described Himself with these words: gracious, compassionate, slow to anger, abounding in lovingkindness and truth (Ex. 34:6). If we are to be children of our heavenly Father, we must exhibit these characteristics as well. In this lesson, we are going to see that we are also called to imitate Jesus Christ and become like Him.

Read Hebrews 2:11-18.
This passage explains the reasons God had for taking on flesh and blood and becoming a man. The passage begins in verse 11 by saying that we share the same Father as Jesus Christ.
In v.11, what is Jesus not ashamed to call us?

What does Jesus call His followers in verse 12?

According to v.17-18, why did Jesus have to become like his brethren? What did it accomplish for Him to become a human being?

Jesus became like us so that we could become like Him. He entered into the human experience of physical suffering and temptation so that He could relate to us in our weakness. After He experienced and successfully overcame all possible temptations, He sacrificed His life for us on the cross. He then was raised from the dead, victorious over Satan, sin, and death – everything that man had been powerless over in the past.

Read John 20:17.
This conversation occurs just after Jesus' resurrection. How does Jesus describe His relationship to His disciples?

How does He describe His disciple's relationship to God?

This is a change in the relational dynamics between Jesus and his disciples. Before the cross, Jesus was Master and Teacher and Lord. Now He is Brother. Both Hebrews 2 and John 20 have the same tone. Jesus is excited to call us brothers and sisters. He has paid dearly for our adoption into His Father's family. He welcomes us in and bids us take our places alongside Him. Do we ever stop to consider our salvation in these terms? It is a great act of love that the Father would call us His children (1 John 3:1); but it is an equally great act of love that Jesus would call us brothers and sisters.

Read Romans 8:14-17.
This passage describes our salvation as God sees it.
What are we who have been born of God called in v.14?

Verse 15 tells us that our status in God's household is NOT that of a _____ but rather as a _____'_____.

What does the Spirit of God within us communicate to our spirits (v.16)?

As God's children, what are we also, according to v.17?

An heir is one who stands to inherit the entire estate of the father. This passage tells us that we are fellow-heirs of God the Father's possessions, alongside Jesus. Can you even wrap your mind around the gracious heart of God? He adopts His enemies and makes them not just servants but sons, fellow heirs with the Perfect Son, Jesus Himself (Gal. 4:7).

When we spoke of imitating God in the previous lesson, we did so in the context of our being His beloved children. We bear His likeness because He is our Father. Now, as we begin to study how to imitate Jesus, let's keep it in the context of His being our older brother – one whom we look up to, admire, and long to emulate.

What is Jesus Like?

As we saw in the previous lesson, in Exodus 34 God tells us in His own words exactly what He is like. In the New Testament we have a similar passage where Jesus describes Himself just as succinctly.

Read Matthew 11:28-30.
In verse 29, Jesus calls us to learn from Him. What does He say He is like?

Out of all the characteristics Jesus could have emphasized about Himself, He chooses gentleness and humility. He bids us to join Him in His yoke, to bind ourselves to Him, and to mimic these qualities.

Getting the Picture

As we look more closely at the gentleness and humility Jesus invites us to share with Him, keep the picture of a yoke in mind. Jesus chose this metaphor deliberately. In our culture, yokes are not a familiar sight, but to Jesus' audience they were as common as pickup trucks. To be in a yoke meant to share the burden of the work. It meant to pull in the same direction toward a common goal. And, most of all, it meant to be side by side, shoulder to shoulder – together.

Jesus accused the religious teachers of His day of laying heavy burdens on the shoulders of the people and not lifting a finger to help them carry them. (Matt. 23:4) Jesus' offer was a stark contrast. Rather than heaping a load of expectations on the backs of His followers, He offers to get into a yoke with them, working right alongside them to do the Father's will. In other words, Jesus is not asking His disciples to do anything that He is not willing to do Himself.

Gentleness

As followers of Christ, we are to imitate His gentle spirit. The Greek word *prautes* translated "gentle" (or "meek") in this passage is fraught with layers of meaning that are lost in the English translation. Since it is so important that we fully understand this word, I am going to quote the entire entry from Zodhiates' *Word Study Dictionary*:

> Meekness, but not in man's outward behavior only, nor in his relations to his fellow man or his mere natural disposition. Rather, it is an inwrought grace of the soul, and the expressions of it are primarily toward God. It is that attitude of spirit [by which] we accept God's dealings with us as good and do not dispute or resist. *Prautes*, according to Aristotle, is the middle standing between two extremes, getting angry without reason, and not getting angry at all. Therefore, *prautes* is getting angry at the right time, in the right measure, and for the right reason. *Prautes* is not readily expressed in English (since the term "meekness" suggests weakness), but it is a condition of mind and heart which demonstrates gentleness, not in weakness, but in power. It is a balance born in strength of character. (p. 1209)

This definition includes two main elements: a disposition toward God and a perspective on anger. When gentleness (or meekness) defines both of these, our character will have both resilience and balance. To get a handle on what this looks like in practice, we are going to take a brief look at a both a sheep and a shepherd.

Gentle -- Like a Sheep

According to Thayer's lexicon, a gentle spirit means "we accept all God's dealings with us as good and do not dispute or resist." Jesus exhibited this characteristic when He came to earth to live and to die for our salvation. When we think of Jesus' gentleness in connection with His death, we usually picture the lamb being led to the slaughter.

Read Isaiah 53:7.
How is Jesus described?

This certainly is the epitome of gentleness. But it is not the whole picture. Turn back a few pages and read Isaiah 50:5-9.
In chapter 53 we picture Jesus as a victim. In chapter 50, who is seen to be in charge?

In chapter 53, the voice is passive. The lamb is led. The lamb is sheared. The lamb is killed. But in chapter 50, the voice is active. Jesus says, "I gave them my back to scourge. I gave them my beard to pluck out and my face to spit upon." Jesus was not a victim. It was His choice to submit to the will of the Father and go to the cross. He was willingly "obedient unto death (Phil.2:8)."

Who was Jesus trusting as He experienced all this? (v.7)

According to Matthew 26:52-53, what could Jesus have done when the soldiers came to arrest Him?

Even while He was being taken to His death, Jesus had absolute power; but His gentleness held Him back from using that power. His gentleness was the quality that allowed Him to rest in the good will and plan of the Father, even as He went to the cross. That same power of gentleness is available to us in the midst of the hardships we find ourselves in.

Read Romans 8:28-39.
In v.29, what relationship do we bear to Christ?

In v.31, who is "for us"?

What kinds of trials are listed in v.35?

Notice in v.36, Paul identifies with Jesus, often feeling like a sheep being led to slaughter himself. But according to v.37, does Paul see himself as a victim?

Why not? What is Paul placing all his hope in, according to v.38-39?

No matter what kind of trials we are experiencing (sickness, danger, poverty, mistreatment), we can face them with the gentleness of a lamb but the power of a conquering warrior because of the love of God in Christ. A gentle spirit enables us to say, "If God is FOR us, does it really matter who is against us?"

Gentle – Like a Shepherd

Every good character quality has an opposite which is like a negative image – a reversal of the good. Gentleness is no exception. The quality of gentleness, if distorted, could become a weak passivity. This is what Aristotle meant when he spoke of two extremes: getting angry without good reason and never getting angry at all. Some things ought to make us angry. Some things ought to stir us to action. If nothing can get our heart pumping and blood boiling, then we are not fully entering into the yoke of Jesus.

Jesus' anger was the anger of a shepherd. Does that sound like an odd comparison to make? Let me show you what I mean.
Imagine a shepherd, sitting under a shade tree on a hillside, watching his sheep. From time to time, he gets up and leads the flock to fresh pasture or to still waters to drink. There by the stream, the shepherd perches on a rock, pulls out a notebook and writes some poetry. Late in the day, he rounds up the sheep, carefully counts them, and sets out on the smooth pathway toward home. Suddenly a wolf darts into view and runs toward the lambs. The serene mood is shattered. The shepherd races toward the beast. He catches up to it and beats it to death with his rod, rescuing the precious lamb from its jaws.

An unlikely story? Not really.
Read 1 Samuel 17:34-35.
What did young David do when he was a shepherd tending his father's sheep?

In 1 Samuel 13:14, Samuel is speaking to King Saul about David, who will become king after him. What phrase does Samuel use to describe David? What kind of a man is he?

One of the names for Jesus was the Son of David (Matthew 1:1). This speaks of His identity in more ways than one. Jesus was a Son of David in that He descended from David's genealogy. But Jesus also identified with David because they had much in common. God chose David to rule Israel because David was a kindred spirit with God in many ways. He made a fitting king because he had a shepherd's heart. He was both gentle and fierce depending on what the situation called for. He was just the kind of shepherd that Jesus would be.

Many Old Testament prophesies about Jesus refer to Him as a shepherd.
Read Isaiah 40:11.
What does the Lord, our Shepherd, do?

Read Isaiah 42:1-3.
This passage describes Jesus, the Servant of God. What is He like?
Read John 10:1-18.
What does Jesus call Himself in v.11?

What does a good shepherd do for His sheep (v.11)?

What kinds of things endanger the sheep (v.8, 12)?

Jesus was gentle toward sinners, compassionate toward the sick, kind to the outcasts, but fierce toward the religious leaders. He referred to false teachers as "ravenous wolves" (Matt.7:5). He warned His disciples about the hypocrisy of the Pharisees (Luke 12:1) and denounced them harshly (Matt. 12:34), calling them evil broods of vipers. He even pronounced "woes" upon them (Matt.23), calling down God's judgment on them and assuring them they would not escape the sentence of hell (Matt.23:33). The reason Jesus was so harsh toward them was that they placed heavy burdens on men's shoulders (Matt. 23:4) and hindered people from coming to God (23:13).

We are to follow Christ's example, exhibiting this kind of balance. As we share His yoke, we are to be characteristically gentle yet righteously angry when the situation calls for it.

Read Jude 1:20-23.
What approach to people are we to take in v.22?

What approach is implied by v.23?

Read Galatians 6:1.
It is interesting how often the language of shepherding comes through in the epistles. Notice this verse speaks of one being "caught" in a trespass. The image is that of a sheep caught in a thicket, stuck and unable to free itself.
What are we to do if we see a brother caught in a sin?

How are we to do it?

Read James 5:19-20.
Again we see the language of sheep. This time the picture is of a brother "straying" from the truth, wandering off and getting lost in the winding paths of false teaching.
What are we to do for such a brother?

As we enter Christ's yoke, abiding in Him, we will find our passions conforming to His. On the one hand, we will have a mild disposition that is not easily angered. But on the other hand, when our brothers or sisters are in danger -- either ensnared by sin or waylaid by the message of a false teacher, we will spring into action. Spurred on by a true spirit of gentleness, we will do everything we can to rescue them. In so doing we, like David, will be people "after God's own heart."

Humility

Jesus not only describes Himself as gentle, but as humble in heart. The Greek word translated "humble" in this verse is *tapeinos*. It means "not rising far from the ground, lowly, of low degree, deferring servilely to others." It speaks of lowness of social position, poverty. It is the exact opposite of the boastful pride of life that our world values and that Satan tempts us toward incessantly.

Humility was the very essence of Jesus' life on earth. Again we see that Jesus never asks us to do anything that He has not done Himself already. None of us will ever be asked to lower ourselves more than Jesus did because none of us has ever started so high!

Read Philippians 2:1-8.
According to verse 5, whose attitude are we to imitate?

What was Jesus' attitude toward His position of equality with God in heaven before He became a baby? (v.6)

What did Jesus do? (v.7)

According to v.7-8, how did Jesus exhibit His humility? (You should find at least three ways.)

As we follow Jesus' example in humility, how are we supposed to view others? (v.3)

As we copy Jesus' attitude, how will we behave? (v.4)

Jesus' humility showed both in His **_practice of service_** toward man and in His **_posture of submission_** to the Father.

Practice of Service

It would be impossible for us to cover all of the ways in which Jesus served humanity. As John said at the end of His gospel, if all Jesus' acts were to be recorded the whole world could not contain the volumes that would have to be written. But this study is all about getting the general picture of essential truths. So, let's just look at a day in the life of Jesus.

Read Mark chapter 1 carefully, and try to picture Jesus' activities as they are described.

In v.17-20, what does Jesus do?

In v.21-22, what does He do?

In v.23-26, what does Jesus do?

In v.29-31, what does He do?

By v.32, what time of day is it?

In v.32-34, what does He do?

According to v.33-35, how much sleep do you think Jesus had that night?

What did Jesus do in v.35?

What happens next goes right to my heart. After the day you just read about, Jesus is trying to have a little bit of time alone with His Father. He must need to be refreshed and recharged after such an exhausting day of ministry. As he is alone in a desolate place, along comes Peter with these words: "Everyone is looking for you!" Immediately my mind goes to my own experiences. I have five children. Occasionally, I slip off to my room and lock the door. I want to read or pray or rest or do a bit of all three. Inevitably, before too long there is a bang on my door. "Mom, what are you doing in there? We've been looking for you! We need you." And just as everything in me wants to shout, "Go away! I need to rest!" I think of Jesus, interrupted during His early morning devotions by immature disciples and a needy crowd.

According to v.38, what is Jesus' response?

In v.39, what is He doing?

In v. 40-42, what does Jesus do?

You get the picture. This went on for three years. Day after day after day, Jesus went about among pressing crowds teaching, healing, touching, loving, serving, serving, serving. Mark goes on like this chapter after chapter.

How does Jesus summarize his mission in Mark 10:45? What did He come to do?

As we join Jesus, our elder brother, in His yoke, we will find ourselves called to a life of this kind of service as well. But remember, it is a yoke. We do not serve alone. We serve in His strength following His example. And Jesus promises that His yoke is easy and His burden light.

Read 2 Corinthians 12:15.
How does Paul describe his feeling about his life of sacrifice in service to the Corinthian believers?

Paul loved sharing a yoke with His Savior. He loved what he called the "fellowship of His sufferings (Phil. 3:10)." When Paul suffered while carrying out the work of Christ on earth, He rejoiced. The call to share Jesus' yoke of humility in the practice of service to others is not a call to misery, but to joy.

Posture of Submission

Jesus' humility also showed itself in His posture of submission. This is a posture we are asked to assume as well, if we are to truly imitate Christ.

Remember we learned that Jesus' gentleness was seen most clearly in how He did not make use of the power that He had at His disposal for selfish ends? Similarly, Jesus' exercise of submission is all the more significant because of Who He really is.

Read John 13:3-5.
What did Jesus know? (v.3)

After reflecting upon what He knew about Himself, what did Jesus do? (v.5)

Again, in our world's kingdom's mindset, this makes absolutely no sense. A person who knows their own greatness does not then stoop to do the work of the lowest household slave. But Jesus does. And it is His yoke we are invited to carry.

Look at 1 Peter 2:5, 9.
How are Christians described in these verses? Who and what are we?

Immediately after establishing that we are of royal blood in God's kingdom, Peter gives a series of commands. Record the commands in each verse below.

2:13

2:17

2:18

3:1

3:7

3:8-9

Whose example are we to be following? (2:21)

It is too easy to pass quickly by these types of verses. Think about that for a moment. Christ "left you an example that you should follow in His steps." Several decades ago, a man named Charles Sheldon took this verse seriously and really thought about what it would look like to live each day walking in the footsteps of Jesus. He wrote a novel called *In His Steps* which reflects his application of this principle. More recently the WWJD (What would Jesus do?) bracelet phenomenon has revived this idea. Unfortunately, when these types of things go commercial they become just another slogan – not something to take seriously. Stop for a minute and just apply the truth of Jesus' example to yourself in the area of submission. Prayerfully consider the verses above and write down what He shows you about your own heart.

Am I submissive in the attitudes of my heart as well as in my actions toward:

- Civil authorities and people who make the rules I am to live by?

- The elected officials in my country, including my President?

- My boss or supervisor at work – whether they are good and fair or not?

- My husband?

- Other believers in general and church leadership specifically?

Remember, if Jesus could place Himself under the authority of flawed, sinful men, so can we! He set us an example so that we would follow in His steps.

Let's look at a final example of Christ's humility.

Read Luke 17:7-8.
In the normal way of things in this world's kingdom, when a slave comes in from the field having worked hard all day, what does the master say to him?

Now read Luke 12:37.
Here Jesus is speaking of His kingdom, the kingdom of Heaven. What is Jesus saying that He will do when He finds His servants faithfully working at His return?

It is one thing to picture Jesus during His short life on earth playing the role of the servant. But Luke 12 speaks of the risen, glorified, returning Lord – not the carpenter's son from Nazareth – girding Himself to wait on tables. Jesus is the same yesterday, today, and forever (Heb. 13:8). This means that the heart of a servant that Jesus displayed during His earthly ministry was not a short-term deviation from His normal Self. The heart of a servant has always characterized our Lord – and our God! This begs the question: If service and submission are not beneath the dignity of the King of Kings and Lord of Lords, how dare we say they are beneath ours?

Again, as we seek to follow Christ's example and walk in His steps, we have to ask ourselves the specific questions. Evaluate your attitude and your service. Am I serving others willingly with a spirit of humility

- At home, both toward my family and in making my home open and available to others?

- In the body of Christ – not just officially in a ministry but in practical availability and helpfulness to individual brothers and sisters wherever needed?

- In the workplace – not just doing my job but looking to serve those I work alongside?

Conclusion

When Jesus specifically bid His followers to learn what He was like, He used these words to describe Himself: "I am gentle and humble in heart" (Matt. 11:29). So, as we seek to imitate Him, these qualities are an excellent starting point. Jesus' gentleness and humility showed up in what He DID do, such as preaching the gospel, casting out demons, healing the sick, and going to the cross. They also showed up in what He did NOT do, such as acting on His own interest to meet His own needs or defend His own honor – or even save His own life. Just as graciousness and compassion color every act of the Father, gentleness and humility color every act of the Son. We are to follow the example of Both – imitating our Father and our Brother.

In every Scripture passage we have examined in the past two lessons, we have seen that the commands given to us and demands made of us have been in the context of our family relationship to God and Christ. We are not asked to do or be anything that God is not already doing and being. As we walk with God and abide in Christ, we take on the characteristics we have studied. Our high position in His family – adopted children and joint-heirs with Christ – gives us the power and the confidence to lower ourselves, as Christ did. We can serve others because we have nothing to prove. We can sacrifice for others because we have nothing to lose.

Matters for Prayer

Spend some time thanking Jesus for welcoming you so enthusiastically into His Father's household. Thank Him for eagerly sharing His inheritance with you. Marvel at the fact that He calls you brother or sister unashamedly. Confess to Him the terrible pride that has caused you at times to be ashamed of Him!

Talk to Jesus about that gentleness and humility He is calling you to join Him in. If it scares you to take up that yoke, tell Him that. Confess all the things that keep you from wanting to take it up.

Pray that Jesus will form His gentleness in you -- that you will be gentle like a sheep, accepting God's will for you without complaining or resisting; and gentle like a shepherd, slow to anger yet quick to rescue a brother in need. Pray that Jesus will form His humility in you -- that you will assume the practice of a servant and the posture of submission.

Ask Him to show you if you are a person who seeks to be served rather than to serve. If so, ask Him to give you insight into how He wants you to follow in His steps and change.

Ask for strength to leave behind the way of thinking that this world's kingdom has programmed into you all your life. Ask God to help you to believe that His way is best, that His yoke truly is easy. Ask for the grace to share joyfully in the fellowship of Christ's sufferings so that one day you can gladly share His glory (Romans 8:17).

Lesson Five

Returning to Titus: Portraits of Christ

In Lesson One, we took a broad look at the book of Titus. We called Titus "a little book of big pictures" because it paints several portraits for us, illustrating what a godly person should be like. In Lesson Two, we learned that in order to think and act like Christians should, we must first realize that we are now citizens of a different kingdom. This kingdom has opposite values, opposite motivations, and opposite priorities from the kingdom of this world. A shift must occur in our entire perspective on life in order for us to fit into this new kingdom. In Lesson Three, we learned that we are not just part of a new kingdom; we are part of a new family – God's family. God expects us to imitate Him as loving children will imitate a parent. We are to strive to become like God Himself in the ways that we studied – His holiness, graciousness, and compassion. Finally, in Lesson Four, we saw that as God's children, we are also Christ's siblings. He is our older Brother. He paves the way for us and sets an example for us to follow. We are to enter into His yoke with Him and learn from Him, copying His gentle and humble character. In this lesson, we are going to return to the book of Titus and take a closer look at the portraits we find there. But before we do that, let's remind ourselves of some important truths.

A Word of Warning

In the Preface to this study, I reminded you that this material must never be separated from what we learned about nurturing the Spirit-born life in *Right From the Start*. I hope you are continuing to use the sheet entitled "For Meditation and Review" as a safeguard against forgetting those key principles. If you are not continuing to nurture your spiritual life by feeding on the life of Christ, taking Him in through His Word, being filled with His Spirit, abiding in Him as a branch in a vine, then you will fall into a dangerous trap in seeking to apply what we are learning now.

The metaphor of the yoke carries with it a certain danger. If we focus on entering into Jesus' yoke with Him without remembering the metaphor of the vine and its branches (John 15), we may come to see our Christian life as a partnership – a 50/50 split. Jesus helps me, but I am working alongside Him too. Jesus contributes His strength, I contribute mine. This would be a serious mistake. If we remember that we are simply a branch on a vine, we will realize that our life is His life. What we bring to Jesus' yoke is the Spirit-born life of God, which He Himself gave us. We do not yoke our fleshly human nature to Christ's Spiritual nature and work alongside Him for God's kingdom. It is only the newly created life of God in us that can fit into Christ's yoke and work with Him to do the Father's will. Remember, all that we offer to God comes from Him and through Him before we can give it back to Him (Romans 11:36).

Two unequal animals cannot share a yoke. You cannot yoke a donkey with an ox. The donkey's legs would dangle uselessly in the air, and it would be nothing but a hindrance to the ox accomplishing its work. That would be a fitting picture of you or me trying to join our old selves to Christ. It simply can't be done.

Portraits of Christ

In Lesson One, we made some lists of character qualities from the book of Titus. Now we are ready to see these lists for what they really are: portraits of Christ.

If Jesus were a …

In the book of Titus, Paul addresses various categories of people, organized according to age, gender, and role in society. He describes how these people should conduct themselves in order to reflect well upon the gospel. Paul explains that by our behavior, we either adorn (2:10) or dishonor (2:5) the Word of God. Now that we have seen that our Christian walk is supposed to be a lifestyle of imitation – of both God and Jesus Christ – we can more fully understand why this is true. People will judge what God is like by how we behave. They will evaluate the power and truth of Jesus by how we live and speak.

Basically, what Paul does in the book of Titus is to show us Jesus in various contexts. If Jesus were an older man, He would be temperate, dignified, sensible, sound in faith, in love, and in perseverance. If He were an older woman, He would be reverent, not a gossip, not enslaved to wine, teaching what is good. If He were a young mother in her home, He would be sensible, pure, a good housekeeper, kind, and submissive. If He were a young man, He would be sensible. If Jesus were a slave (or an employee in any job), He would be submissive to His boss, not argumentative, not stealing from His employer, but working hard in good faith. And, finally, if Jesus were a citizen of any country on earth, He would be subject to civil authorities, obedient to the laws, ready to do good. He would not speak against His leaders. He would be uncontentious, gentle, and considerate to all men.

When we see these lists in this way, they come to life. They are no longer sterile checklists or rules to live by. They are living and active, penetrating words. They bring Christ near to each of us and help us to identify with Him. These lists are exciting and helpful to us as we seek to mimic our Father and Brother right where we live.

A close examination of these lists quickly reveals several points where they overlap. Some characteristics appear again and again. They do not fall neatly into categories of role and gender. For example, the call to submission applies both to women in their homes and to men in their workplaces. The command to be sensible applies both to older men and to younger women. This makes sense because all these traits belong to Christ; and Christ's character does not change based on His environment. He is Who He is, no matter what context He finds Himself in. For this reason, we are not going to study these qualities according to category. We are going to study the traits that emerge repeatedly and apply to every Christian, everywhere.

As we look at several of these traits, let us remember we are looking at Christ. Our goal is to look into the mirror at ourselves -- whether we are young or old, men or women, workers or citizens – and see Christ clearly reflected there (2 Corinthians 3:18).

Sensible

Of all the character traits dealt with in Titus, this one gets the most emphasis. The Greek word translated "sensible" appears five times in Titus.
WHO is told to be sensible in each of the following verses? (If necessary, read the surrounding verses for context.)

Titus 1:8

Titus 2:2

Titus 2:5

Titus 2:6

Titus 2:12

This word is *sophron*, and it means "of sound mind, self-controlled, moderate as to opinion or passion." According to Zodhiates' lexicon, it means to be discreet, sober, of a sound mind. It describes a person who follows sound reasoning and restrains his passions.

Why the emphasis?

Proverbs 23:7 tells us, "As a man thinks in his heart, so is he." Our thinking shapes everything about ourselves. There is tremendous power in right thinking and incalculable danger in wrong thinking. That is why it is so vital that we be of sound mind, sensible in every respect.

Sense and Sensibility in Proverbs

A good place to start in understanding what it means to be sensible is the book of Proverbs. (If you are using the NASB translation, the English word for sensible is "prudent.")

Read the following and write in your own words what the sensible (or prudent) person does or does not do. Notice that Proverbs are often paired ideas. One half of the verse may describe the opposite of the other half. This can be helpful in discerning the meaning of the proverb.

Prov.12:16

Prov. 13:16

Prov. 14:8

Prov. 14:15

Prov. 15:5

The Proverbs paint a picture of a sensible person. The sensible person is not ruled by his passions. He does not lose his temper and make a fool of himself. He thinks before he acts. He carefully plans and gives thought to his decisions. He is not gullible or easily deceived. He accepts correction and learns from it.

When people lack sense, they live on a slippery slope. They are a danger to themselves and others. When people who claim the name of Christ lack sense, they cause the gospel of God to be maligned.

Consider this passage and record the characteristics of men and of women in the chart below.

People who lack sense- 2 Timothy 3:1-5	Women who lack sense- 2 Timothy 3:6-7

A Depraved Mind

People who lack sense are said to have a "depraved mind" (v.8). The men in the passage are characterized by recklessness and pleasure-seeking. They are lovers of themselves, loud, boastful, and arrogant. In the midst of our self-promoting, entertainment-crazed, thrill-seeking culture, Paul's words to Timothy hardly seem to have been written nearly 2000 years ago.

Women who lack sense are characterized by gullibility, guilt complexes, and an all-encompassing discontentment. They are ever seeking and never finding. Again, this rebuke speaks loudly to us today. Browsing a bookstore – whether Christian or secular – reveals the endless quests of women. Women seek answers to marital struggles, parenting issues, and financial problems. They seek solutions to problems of managing their time, their weight, their relationships, and their closets. They seek relief from emotional problems like depression, anxiety, and even boredom. The sheer abundance of books, magazines, and blogs devoted to these issues demonstrate plainly that women today are "ever seeking but never able to come to the knowledge of the truth" in just about every area of their lives.

According to Zhodiates' *Word Study Dictionary*, the opposite of being sensible is to be "foolish, rash, mindless, unthinking, possessed with a demon, demon-like."
Read Mark 5:1-15.
What is this man like before Jesus casts the demons out of him?

What is he like in v.15?

Before His encounter with Jesus, who controlled this man's mind?

We may think this has very little to do with us. After all, how many of us have ever run howling and naked through the wilderness, cutting ourselves with stones and breaking chains with our bare hands? We may find it hard to believe that before we came to the knowledge of Christ, we, too, were bound by Satan in a kind of insanity – perhaps less dramatic than that of the demoniac, but still just as real.

Read 2 Timothy 2:22-26.
What do those who have been "held captive by Satan to do his will" need, according to v.25? (2 things)

Notice the similar phrasing in 2 Timothy 2:25-26 and 3:7. Both speak of "coming to a knowledge of the truth" as the way one "comes to their senses."

Satan lies to the subjects of his kingdom constantly. He tells them hundreds if not thousands of lies each and every day through various types of media. A person with no knowledge of God is out of touch with reality in that they do not know the truth about the most basic issues of life. As people who have a relationship with Jesus, we should be characterized by sanity and good sense. In a world where people often let their passions rule their actions, we should display an evenness of temperament. When many around us fall prey to fears, anxiety, or even just confusion, we should have clarity of thought and balance of perspective. By being sane and sensible in a world that often seems to have gone mad, we can shine as lights and reflect well on the power and sufficiency of the message of Christ.

The tragedy is that many Christians today are not beacons of sanity. They are prey to the same issues that enslave their unsaved friends and neighbors. They have no firmer grasp on the realities of the kingdom of God than the lost. They are, in many cases, the blind leading the blind.

If we, as Christians, have any love for people and any concern for the reputation of the gospel, we should seriously seek to be sensible people. As sensible people we will be able to offer real, practical help to others. We will also demonstrate the power and truth of God's Word in the context of the practical issues of life. This adorns the gospel of God.
So, how do we become sensible people?

Sensibility and the Spirit of Christ

Turn to Isaiah 11. This passage is a prophecy describing Jesus, the Messiah, who would be born many hundreds of years after this passage was written. Verse 2 describes the Spirit of Jesus Christ. List 6 phrases from this verse that describe the Spirit.

Verse 3 goes on to describe the sound judgment of Christ, explaining that He would not judge things based on appearances but according to righteousness and truth.

This is the Spirit of Christ. The Holy Spirit, Who was in Christ, is characterized by wisdom, understanding, strength, counsel, knowledge, the fear of the Lord, and sound judgment.

Read Romans 8:9-11.
Where is the Spirit of Christ today?

This is a very important concept to grasp. This same Spirit is within each and every true believer in Jesus Christ! *But do we live in the light of this truth?*

When we need wisdom to sort out a conflict, where do we turn instinctively? To a friend? A parent? A book? A web site? When we need strength to persevere through a stressful day, where do we turn? Facebook? The fridge? When we need more knowledge of God's principles, where do we go? Christian radio? Church? When we are lacking in sound judgment, do we even realize it? Our Christian culture in America is so glutted with replacements for the Spirit of Christ that we often turn to Him only as a last resort, if at all.

Remember the women who are "ever seeking and never coming to the knowledge of the truth"? They seek everything they think is required to be successful in their lives and in their homes, while all the time everything they need is waiting right at hand.

Read Proverbs 14:1.
Who builds her house?

Read Proverbs 24:3-4.
What are the three building materials required for a wise woman to build her home?

Where is a woman to get these materials?
(Refer back to Isaiah 11:2)

I am blessed with a very wise Christian mother. But she did not become wise automatically. When I started kindergarten, my mother thought that would be a perfect time for her to go back to college and finish her teaching degree. As she sought God's will concerning this, she was certain that God was leading her not to go back to school, but rather to spend all the hours she would have spent in classes studying His Word instead. That is exactly what she did. She brought my sister and me to school each morning then went to the library and studied her Bible until it was time to bring us home. In the process she discovered what the Psalmist describes in Ps. 119:99, "I have more insight than all my teachers, for Your testimonies are my meditation." My mother acquired a practical, real-life wisdom that has blessed many over the years. But the ironic thing is, despite having this wonderful source of wisdom so close at hand, I almost never go to my mother for advice! The most valuable thing I learned from her was to go to God directly and seek wisdom first hand from His Spirit and His Word.

Read Proverbs 2:1-6.
Where do wisdom, understanding, and knowledge come from?

How does one get these things? (notice the verbs)

This passage reflects how actively we are to pursue the wisdom of God. Our seeking should be described by words like digging, searching, crying aloud. We seek it with purpose and direction. But the place where we do this seeking is in the Word of God and in prayer – not browsing the bookstore or the internet. Don't misunderstand; there is a place for learning from others. We don't always have to reinvent the wheel. We can get tips and ideas from other sources. But our hearts must be inclined to seek God first, to go to Him for wisdom, to abide in the Spirit of Christ which is the Spirit of wisdom, understanding, and knowledge. It is too easy to depend on other people and ignore the Spirit of God. It is too easy to drown out His voice with countless other voices. How great is our loss when we do!

But what if the sources we go to for wisdom are godly and biblical? What if their advice is sound? That may be true. We may be able to get the correct answers from other people, but we cannot get the power to act on that truth from them. The power to act on what we learn comes only through the Spirit of God. Other people may be able to give us guidance, but they cannot make us follow their advice. Only God can change our hearts. Only His Spirit can give us both the desire and the power to obey (Phil. 2:13).

Summing up Sensibility

So, what have we learned?

- To be sensible means to be reasonable, sound, and solid in one's thinking
- Sensibility is the trait most emphasized in Titus, being specifically cited in the context of church leaders, men, women, and Christians in general
- A sensible person is a thinking person, not ruled by emotions or whims, not gullible or easily led astray
- A sensible person is NOT characterized by seeking without finding – seeking pleasure, thrills, happiness, and answers where there is nothing of lasting worth to be found
- A sensible person is one who is filled with the Spirit of Christ and possesses wisdom, understanding, and knowledge, sound judgment, good counsel, and the fear of the Lord
- A sensible person goes to God directly for wisdom – seeking Him diligently and deliberately in prayer and in study of the Word
- A sensible person adorns the Word of God by proving that it is powerful, relevant, and more than adequate in every situation

What would it look like to apply what we've learned? Take some time to carefully evaluate the following:

- Am I sensible (reasonable, moderate) or am I ruled by my emotions? Do I think before I act or do I act without thinking?
- Am I a weak-willed woman, at the mercy of my own desires?
- Am I burdened by guilt because I live in a perpetual state of sin, lacking discipline in the basic areas of my life?
- Am I in a constant quest for answers and solutions to my problems, but never finding anything that "works"?
- Where do I seek comfort and help?
- How often do I go to God personally and directly for wisdom?

According to 2 Timothy 2:25, if we lack sensibility we need to go to God and repent of these sins. We need to ask Him to grant us knowledge of the truth. Ask Him to bring us to our senses so we can escape the Devil's traps and be free to do God's will – not Satan's. That is our first and only hope. After that, we pursue wisdom through the Spirit of wisdom by spending much time alone with God in His Word. There is no secret, no substitute, no shortcut, no method other than that!

"If any of you lacks wisdom, he should ask God, who gives to all generously and without criticizing, and it will be given to him." James 1:5

Sound

The quality of soundness is closely related to that of being sensible. To be sound means to be whole and healthy. When used in its literal sense, this word refers to physical health (Luke 7:10; 3 John 1:2). But most frequently in Scripture, the word *sound* is used metaphorically. In the following passages, write down what is described as being "sound."

1 Timothy 6:3 and 2 Timothy 1:13

2 Timothy 4:3 and Titus 1:9, 2:1

Titus 1:13 and 2:2

As Christians, soundness should describe our words, our doctrine, and our faith. These should be good and wholesome through and through.

Sound Words

Read Proverbs 18:21.
What power is found in the tongue?

Read Proverbs 12:18.
What does the tongue of the wise bring?

Read Ephesians 4:15.
What kind of words are we to speak?

Read Colossians 4:6.
What is our speech to be like?

Read Ephesians 4:29.
What kinds of words are we to speak?

This final verse is particularly interesting for the contrast it offers. The word "unwholesome" is the opposite of "soundness." According to *Strong's Dictionary and Lexicon*, it means "rotten, putrefied, corrupted and no longer fit for use, of poor quality, worthless." If we were honest, we might be forced to admit that many of our words could be described this way.

Read James 3:8-12.

Should it be possible for the same mouth to bless God but curse men?

When people observe this kind of double standard in our lives, are we adorning the Word of God or dishonoring it?

Jesus' words were always appropriate to the moment. He always knew what to say to each person who came His way. He had gentle words for some and harsh words for others, but He always told the truth in love.

Read John 12:49 and John 14:10.

How did Jesus know what to say?

Read Isaiah 50:4.

What kinds of words did the Father teach Jesus to speak?

Remember, Jesus is our example. Jesus rose early each morning and met with God. He listened as a disciple would listen and learned what to say in order that He might sustain the weary ones with His words. If God would do this for Jesus, surely He would also do this for us, if we would seek Him the way that Jesus did.

Ask yourself, how seriously do you take your words? Do you see them as agents of healing or of destruction, as they are portrayed in Proverbs and James? Do you see them as the measure of the purity of your faith — or else the place where you discover your own hypocrisy? If your words are a mixture of bitter water and sweet, if you bless God and curse men with the same tongue, confess that to the Lord and ask Him to help you become sound in your speech.

Sound Doctrine

Not only are our words to be sound, but our doctrine is to be sound as well. Doctrine is the solid set of truths upon which we build our lives.

Read Matthew 7:24-27.

Look carefully at verses 24 and 26. What was the only difference between the two builders?

Every one of us is a life-builder. We make decisions and perform actions and speak words every single day of our lives. Some people base their decisions and actions on their own common sense, their upbringing, their education, or the example of others. Those people are building their lives on the sand. Eventually a storm will come that will sweep all that away and show it for what it was — a house with no foundation. Others base their decisions, words, and actions on the doctrines (or truths) of the Bible. They hear the word of God, and they obey it. These people will also experience the storms of life, but their lives will not be destroyed by them. They have built upon a rock.

We sometimes have the idea that doctrine is theoretical knowledge – classroom stuff that is impractical in every-day life. That could not be farther from the truth. Each believer should have a solid foundation of doctrine underneath them that literally forms the basis for everything they do. For example:

- The doctrine of God- This means knowing Who God is and what He is like. Knowing God's character is essential to coping with and processing life's difficulties. How can we love or trust Someone we do not really know?
- The doctrine of Man- This means understanding who and what we are as human beings. Where did we come from? Why did God make us? Why are we in the condition we are in today? What can we expect from people apart from God? What are the real human needs? If we don't understand these things, we will not know how to relate to one another constructively. We will find ourselves pouring our energy into all the wrong goals, doing one another more harm than good.
- The doctrine of Salvation- This means understanding what Jesus accomplished on the cross and by His resurrection. It means understanding how exactly God can be both just and justifier of sinners. It means understanding the process of sanctification which the Spirit is performing in us every day. If we don't understand our relationship with God, how can we approach Him boldly? If we don't know what He is trying to accomplish in us, how can we cooperate with His work?

Studies have shown that those of us born in the United States are more ignorant of our laws, history, and constitution than those who immigrate and become naturalized citizens. I fear the same is true in the Church. Often those who are raised in Sunday School from infancy know plenty of stories but not much doctrine. We think we know more than we do and are complacent about our study. We don't realize how little we know or understand of the deeper things of God until those storms rock our foundations and we find out how shaky they are.

Read 2 Timothy 2:15-19.
According to v.15, what should every workman of God be able to do?

In v.17, what is false doctrine compared to?

If you have ever seen an old Civil War era movie, you are probably familiar with gangrene. Some poor solder pulls off a boot and reveals an old injury, and you see that his leg is black and rotten. The medic shakes his head, and out comes the saw. Gangrene was a fearsome disease with no cure. This gruesome, horrible image is the one Paul chooses to invoke when he speaks of faulty doctrine.

In v.19, Paul borrows Jesus' metaphor and refers to sound doctrine as "the firm foundation of God." We must know the Scriptures and be able to accurately handle them so that we can build our lives on a good foundation and so that we can help others to do the same.

What are we supposed to be able to do with doctrine, according to Titus 1:9?

What is the command in Titus 2:1?

What kind of doctrine are we to have in Titus 2:8?

Titus 2:10 reminds us of the goal of this study: that we might adorn the doctrine of God by our deeds. When we live consistently with the truths of Scripture, we make the doctrines of God appealing. This brings God glory, and it wins others to faith in the gospel.

Test yourself. Do you have a firm grasp on the basic doctrines of the faith? Most study Bibles have summaries of these doctrines outlined in the back among the notes and resources. Invest some serious time in studying these things and make sure your foundation is solid.

Sound Faith

When we are told to have sound faith, this means we are to have a strong, robust, settled conviction of the truth of what we believe. A sound faith is a solid faith.

Read James 1:6-8.
What is the opposite of faith, in v.6?

How is the person who lacks faith described in v.8?

Read Ephesians 4:14.
How are people who are not sure of their doctrine described?

If sound faith can best be compared to a stone foundation on which to build, these passages give us the exact opposite picture. Those who are not sound in their faith are compared to a little boat driven and tossed on the waves of the sea. They go wherever the wind takes them. They are tied to nothing, sure of nothing, at the mercy of their circumstances.

Read Hebrews 6:17-20.
What is our hope compared to in v.19?

When our hope rests on the unchangeable nature of God and His promises, and our eyes are fixed on Christ who is our forerunner, who blazed the trail for us and showed us the way, we will have a sound faith. Our lives will rest on something solid. We will have an anchor for our souls. This confidence will give us a stability and strength in the midst of life's difficulties which will reflect well on the gospel and prove its truth to those who observe us.

A Sound Mind

"For God has not given us the spirit of fear; but of power, and of love, and of a sound mind." (KJV)

Other translations render "sound mind" with words like "discipline" or "self-control." Neither rendering is complete in itself because the Greek word and its roots imply both "coming to one's senses" and "restraining one's impulses." As such, looking at this word is a fitting bridge between our study of **soundness** and of **self-control** in Titus.

This verse in Timothy gives us an interesting contrast, making fear the opposite of soundness of mind. This is a contrast worth exploring.

I am sure that most of us can relate to feeling somewhat "out of our minds" at times. We can go through our day, mind racing, thoughts out of control. We sometimes lay awake at night and our brains are like a runaway train taking us places we don't want to go. Or perhaps a "voice" plays in our heads like background noise all the time, telling us things, interpreting things for us, making us feel vaguely uneasy all the time.

There are many ways our minds can slip out of control – not just out of our own control, but out of the Holy Spirit's control. We can be guilty of many sins of the mind, each of which is a result of choosing to board a train of thought that we have no business traveling on. And, to stretch the metaphor, many of these trains belong to the same railway: *fear*.

Consider some examples:

- Rationalizing sin – rooted in a fear of not getting what I think will make me happy
- Jealousy or Suspicion – rooted in a fear of being displaced
- Manipulation/Distortion – rooted in a fear of losing control of a person or situation
- Worry/Anxiety – rooted in a fear of loss or harm
- Fantasy – (including pursuit of virtual reality /online identities) – fear of facing my real responsibilities or my real Self
- Negativity (perceiving and portraying everything in the worst possible light) – fear of losing the sympathy (and attention) of others; fear of facing that the "problem" is within ME, not my circumstances
- Paranoia/Pessimism- fear that God is not good or cannot be trusted

None of the above reflects a soundness of mind. None of them does justice to the Spirit which God has placed within us.

When our thoughts spin out of control or we fall into consistent patterns like the ones named above, we need to take decisive action.

Read 2 Corinthians 10:3-5.
Where does our battle take place?

What are we fighting to destroy?

What are we to do to our thoughts?

Read Colossians 3:1-3.
What are we to keep seeking (v.1)?

What are we to set our mind upon (v.2)?

What fact is to shape all our thinking (v.3)?

The Psalms are a textbook on setting the mind and controlling the thoughts. If you struggle with your thoughts, read through the Psalms and notice the following:
- All the references to meditation. Note what the psalmists meditate upon and when they do this. You will notice many references to meditating "through the watches of the night." Nighttime

is when many people's minds get out of control. Anxiety presses in, and all sorts of distorted perspectives take hold. They seem to move in with the darkness and out with the dawn. Take decisive action and meditate on God and His Word during these vulnerable hours.

- <u>The shifts in perspective from the beginning of the Psalm to the end and what caused that shift.</u> Many Psalms begin with a struggle or complaint and end with praise. That is not a coincidence. The act of writing the Psalm functioned as means to take thoughts captive to the Spirit of God. If you aren't a poet, you can use a journal to accomplish the same effect. First put your burdens and thought processes on paper where they can be objectively examined in light of Scripture. Then tell yourself the truth about God and ask Him to bring that truth home to your heart and mind. Finally, praise Him for Who He is!

- <u>The willingness to recognize and confess sinful thought patterns.</u>   The psalmists would not have reached the place of praise if they had hidden from their sinful perspective. For example, in Psalm 73, Asaph began by complaining about the injustice of God. He was not *doing* anything wrong, but his *thinking* had gone very wrong. In the middle of the psalm, he realized that he had been envying sinners for their prosperity. He confessed this sin and got his thinking in proper perspective. At the end of the psalm he could honestly say that the nearness of God was the only good thing he needed in life. Nothing else mattered.

Much (if not all) sin begins in the mind. It is important to remember that sins committed in our thinking are not imaginary – they are just as real as adultery and murder (Matt. 5:22, 28). A lie told to ourselves in our thinking is still a lie, even if we are its only victim. A false image of God in our mind is still an idol. We need to be proactive about our thoughts, taking control of them lest they take control of us. We must treat our minds as the first field of battle in spiritual warfare, bringing every thought into complete subjection to God's truth.

Self-Controlled

To be self-controlled means to have mastery over one's self, particularly one's appetites. It means to master, control, curb, and restrain. Even though this word only appears once in Titus (1:8), it is strongly implied elsewhere in the book.

Read Titus 1:12.
What reputation do the people of Crete have? What are they considered to be like?

Now read v.13-16.
Does it seem from these verses that some who claim to be Christians also have this reputation?

How does this reputation impact their ability to spread the gospel effectively (v.16)?

If Christians lack self-control, we become just like the lost world around us. In a world that gives free rein to every impulse of their flesh, we need to be a different kind of people.
According to Titus 2:12, how are we to live?

Let's look at some aspects of self-control addressed in Titus.

Temperance

Titus 2:2 states that "older men are to be temperate..." Temperance is an old fashioned word for something that is rapidly becoming an old fashioned idea. According to Strong's Greek dictionary, this word means "sober, abstaining from wine, either entirely or at least from its immoderate use."

What command regarding wine is given to the older women in v.3?

For the purposes of application, I think it is fair to say that the emphasis in these passages is not so much on consuming alcoholic beverages as it is on addiction. To be temperate would mean to be free from addiction to any substance. In our current culture, addiction terminology is so common it has lost some of its impact. Addiction is treated as a disease, and ideas about the "cures" abound. The NASB translates the phrase in Titus 2:3, "nor enslaved to much wine." This is a helpful reality check. The word "enslaved" is *douloo* in the Greek. It means "to make a slave of, reduce to bondage."

Read Romans 6:18.
To what should Christians be enslaved?

Read Romans 6:22.
To whom should we be enslaved?

The very heart of the gospel is freedom from bondage to sin and voluntary slavery to God alone. If a Christian is held in the grip of an addiction, the gospel is dishonored. For this reason, we should be characterized by self-control that shows up in freedom from addiction of any kind – not just alcohol, but food, sleep, computer use, anything!

Idolatry

What we call "addiction" Scripture calls idolatry. An addict is a slave to something. The Christian is only to be a slave of Christ, bound to righteousness. Therefore, when a Christian is enslaved to something other than God, that thing is an idol. It has taken the place of God.

In her book *Idols of the Heart*, Elyse Fitzpatrick identifies idols as anything
- you will sin to get
- you will respond sinfully if you do not get.

If we are honest, this will lead us right to the threshold of many a shrine in our hearts! Another writer described idols this way:
- Saying to God: You are negotiable, but this is not.
- Saying to God: I can live without you, but not without this.

For those of us who rely on coffee to start our day, such statements chill the marrow – but they also make us think. We seriously need to evaluate what gets us through the day, what gives us energy, strength, and pleasure? Is it friends? Food? Drink? Exercise? Work? Our computer? Enjoyment wherever we find it?

One way to identify idols is to take the things that are precious to you and "fast" from them in three day periods. Remember, these things are not necessarily sinful in themselves, but they have become sinful if they are indispensable to you. There is no surer way to find out if you are tied to a stake than to start walking. If you hit a point where you just can't take another step away, then that "thing" has you bound. It is an idol. Idols must not be taken lightly. We must tear them down and root them out. But how?

Decades ago a man named Thomas Chalmers made this statement: "The only way to dispossess [the heart] of an old affection is by the expulsive power of a new one." He goes on to explain that we can only be delivered from the tyranny of our heart's former desires by being filled with the Spirit of adoption, by which our spirit cries out, "Abba, Father!" to God and our affection for Him is stronger than our attachment to anything else. That is the Spirit we received the moment of our salvation. But we must cultivate and yield to that Spirit – not quench Him and grieve Him. We must seek God, building our relationship with Him, repenting of the many ways we displace Him, and asking Him to fill us with His own love that we may return it to Him in pure worship.

Too often we go after our idols from the outside-in. We try all sorts of means and methods to break the stronghold of our addictions and get control over our behavior. Long before the invention of self-help books and ten step programs, Paul warned us that this would not work. Colossians 2:21-23 tells us plainly that external restraints on behavior do nothing to change the heart. We will either revert to our sin or we will become inflated with self-righteousness because of our superior will power.

The only way to topple an idol is to become a true worshipper of God – to love Him with all our heart, all our soul, all our mind, and all our strength. That is the expulsive power of a new affection!

Submissive

In Lesson Four we looked briefly at submission when we studied Jesus' example of humility. But there is more that must be said on the subject. The Greek word for submission is *hypotasso* and it means "to arrange under, to appoint, order, ordain." It is chiefly a military term referring to "ranking under" a superior officer.

In the following passages, the same Greek word is used in each case. Don't be confused by any variety in English translation (submit, subject to, obey) because they are all referring to the same thing. For each verse, write down who is to be submissive to whom.

Luke 2:51 (see v.41-51 for context)

1 Corinthians 15:28

James 4:7

Ephesians 5:24

Titus 3:1; Romans 13:1; 1 Peter 2:13

Titus 2:9; 1 Peter 2:18

1 Peter 5:5

Ephesians 5:21

Titus 2:5; Col. 3:18; 1 Peter 3:1

These verses make it clear that Christianity is to be a culture of submission. It is far too common to single out wives and miss the mandate to every other believer. Every Christian, both male and female, is to bear the image of Christ in an attitude of submission toward every God-ordained authority. This includes employers, police officers, government leaders, church elders, and husbands in the home. The passages in which these verses are found make it clear that whether a boss or a government official is fair or unfair, righteous or unrighteous makes no difference. Keep in mind, when Peter wrote the words, "Fear God and honor the emperor," the current emperor of Rome was Nero.

As in everything else, Christ sets us the example. Our older Brother shows us the way. Jesus submitted Himself to His earthly parents. He submitted to Caesar by paying His taxes. He put Himself under the legal authority of numerous corrupt rulers, from the Sanhedrin to Herod and Pilate, when He submitted to a trial that ended in His execution. But above all, He was an obedient Son to His Father.

We know that Jesus is equal to God in every way, made of the same essence, possessing the same attributes. Yet, Jesus did not cling to that equality (Phil.2). Jesus assumed the role of Son in order to accomplish our salvation. He consented to a position lower than the Father for a purpose and for a time.

Read Hebrews 5:8.
What did Jesus learn, according to this verse?

This does not mean that Jesus was disobedient and then He learned obedience. It means that Jesus learned obedience by experiencing a position under authority for the first time when He was made a man. Before the incarnation, Jesus never had to obey – even as God Himself has no one to obey. Part of being born of Mary was becoming a Son – both to Mary and to God. This was a new experience. But Jesus submitted Himself to this arrangement. Now He calls us to do the same. Whether we are wives in the home or employees in the workplace, how can we feel demeaned by being called to fill a position which Christ fills Himself? If He will arrange His life under legitimate authorities, why should we chafe against doing so?

Evaluate your own heart of submission. Do you chafe under authority? Are there areas in your life where you have demanded to be in charge? Does it bother you that God has placed you under the authority of flawed, sinful human beings? Confess this attitude to God honestly and ask Him to fill you more perfectly with the Spirit of Christ. Thank Him that you can identify with Him in this area, just as He was willing to identify with you.

Serve Faithfully

In Titus, Paul has very specific instructions for the worker in the workplace. Admittedly, because of the original culture and audience, the letter refers to slaves and masters. But we can easily extrapolate the truths and apply them to employees and employers in places of business today.

Read Titus 2:9-10.
List the characteristics of the Christ-like worker.

First of all, the employee is to be "well –pleasing." We might say pleasant. He or she is to be an acceptable worker who does their job well. Secondly, the worker is not to be argumentative. He should not talk back or challenge the boss when given a task. Third, the employee should not steal from his boss or the company. Certainly wasting time on the job would be one way of robbing one's employer. An employee should be worthy of his wages. Finally, he should be faithful. His boss should have full confidence that the worker will discharge all his duties thoroughly and well – whether he is being directly supervised or not.

Read Ephesians 6:5-8
According to v.6, when a "slave" renders service to his master, who is he actually serving?

Who should we consider ourselves to be working for (v.7)?

Verse 9 has a word to employers. What kind of boss should a Christian be?

Why?

Read Colossians 3:22-24.
How should we do our work?

Why?

According to Colossians 4:1, what should employers keep in mind?

Conclusion

In this lesson, we took a detailed look at the book of Titus with the intention of seeing Christ's own character displayed in various contexts. We learned the following:

- We are to be sensible, not victims of our own passions or those of others.
- We are to be sound (whole and healthy) in our words, our doctrine, faith, and mind.
- We are to be self-controlled, not addicted or enslaved to anything – free from idols
- We are to be submissive to every authority God has placed over us; and we are simply to be submissive people in general, modeling our attitudes after the example of Christ.
- Finally, we learned that we are to serve faithfully, doing all our work wholeheartedly as service to the Lord Jesus. If we are employees, we are to faithfully serve our employer by working hard for the glory of God. If we are the employers, we are to treat those under us the way we want to be treated by the Lord Himself, remembering that even if we are the boss on earth, we still serve our Master in Heaven.

In each area mentioned above, our motivation in conforming to the example of Christ is to adorn the gospel of God. As we show ourselves to be different from the lost – saner, sounder, more self-controlled, submissive, and faithful in service – we prove that God's Word is true and His ways are best. We silence those who would criticize Christianity by showing that it is a beautiful thing when sincerely practiced.

Matters for Prayer

Begin by praying through the "For Meditation and Review" sheet from Part One. Thank God for your Spirit-born life and for the way the life of Christ nourishes and sustains you as you seek to grow in Him.

Using the summary of this lesson (above),
- *Confess to Christ the areas in which you dishonor God's Word rather than adorning it.*
- *Ask Him to form each of these qualities in you in His way, in His timing, and by His grace.*

Lesson Six

Christ's Reflection in the Home

In Lesson Five, we looked at the book of Titus as a series of portraits of Christ. We studied the positive characteristics that each believer is expected to exhibit as we imitate Christ. We saw that whether man, woman, young, or old, Jesus' example demands that we be sensible, sound, self-controlled, submissive, and faithful in service. In this lesson and the next, we are going to go back into Titus and look specifically at two areas in which we are to imitate Christ and set an example: the home and the workplace. The purpose of these lessons is to bring the truths of Titus right to our doorstep so we can't possibly miss their application.

Please realize this is only a survey of the Bible's teaching on these topics. It would be impossible to treat each one in depth. In fact, whole books have been written on each of the subheadings in this lesson. For our purposes, we will focus exclusively on what it would mean to follow Christ's specific example as a woman in the home.

Jesus in the Home

"Older women likewise are to be reverent in their behavior, not malicious gossips, nor enslaved to much wine, teaching what is good, that they may encourage the younger women to love their husbands and children, to be sensible, pure, workers at home, kind, being subject to their own husbands, that the word of God may not be dishonored." (Titus 2:3-5)

Reverent in their Behavior

The word translated "reverent" in Titus 2:3 is packed with implications. This Greek word *hieroprepes* does not appear anywhere else in the Bible. It is unique to this passage. The root words, however, can be found elsewhere. The word *hieroprepes* is derived from two words. The first means "holy, sacred." It is the same root that is found in the word "temple." The second means "to be suitable or proper." Thus we could say that "reverent" behavior is that which is suitable to holy or sacred service. Jesus modeled this during His entire earthly ministry. He had a clear understanding of His calling, purpose, and mission on earth. Each of us should have the same. He was here to reveal God's nature and do God's will. We are here for the very same purpose. That purpose should set the tone for everything we do.

Attitude of Separation

We learned in a previous lesson that "holy" (or "sacred") means "set apart." Another word for this would be "dedicated." I remember when my church was in the planning stages of their new building, one of their goals was to have a "dedicated nursery." I thought by this they meant they were going to dedicate the nursery to the Lord. It seemed strange to me that they would single out the nursery for dedication when I assumed the whole building would be dedicated to the Lord. I felt a bit foolish when I eventually realized that the phrase really meant that the nursery would not be used for any other purpose other than child care. In the previous building (which also housed a Christian school during the week) it was not uncommon for the nursery to be used for study halls or student gatherings. This meant the room was not kept as safe and sanitary for the babies as it should have been. The "dedicated nursery" would remedy this by being used for nothing but infant care.

We are to consider ourselves to be dedicated to the Lord for His use alone. As women in our home, this means we will do every task as unto the Lord. We will work wholeheartedly, conscious that every small bit of housework or meal preparation is significant to the Lord. As we consider the meaning of the word "reverent," it is interesting to develop the comparison in our minds between the work of a woman in her home and the work of a priest in the temple. Much of what the priests in the temple did was very mundane. They had bread to bake, incense to mix, meat to cook, utensils to wash. If you read the book of Leviticus, you will also find that every rash and scab had to be brought to the priests for examination and treatment. (Does this all sound familiar, Moms?) We often picture the priests only in the context of the lofty work of offering sacrifices or studying the Scriptures. But they were also very simply God's housekeepers. They literally kept His house. As we oversee matters in our home, we are to do so with a wholeheartedness and dedication that reflects well on the Lord we serve.

Tone of Worship

Read Leviticus 10:1-3.
This is a difficult passage to read. Here we see two of Aaron's sons making an offering to the Lord. That seems like a good thing, doesn't it? But yet, it was an offering God did not prescribe or command. They offered it presumptuously. They figured, "We are priests. We can do what we want, when we want." God would not tolerate this.

In v.3, what did God say that gives us insight into what these men did wrong?

These two men dishonored God by their attitude toward Him. They were self-willed, coming on their own terms and not following the very specific regulations for offerings that God had laid down. Because they were priests who represented God to the people, God had to deal particularly harshly with them so that their irreverence would not spread among the people.

In our modern society, it is very tempting to think that we are entitled to do things our own way. God's Word may say that a woman should submit to her husband or be a "keeper at home" or discipline and train her children according to the Scriptures; but everything in our culture teaches us to make our own rules and set our own standards. The advice of the day is, "Well, maybe the Bible says that, but if it doesn't work in your family, try something different." And we do – without a bit of hesitation. Do we ever call this what it is? Irreverence for God? Nadab and Abihu were allowed to offer incense to God under certain circumstances, using fire from a certain altar. But when they launched out and did it their own way, God struck them dead. In our day, we would argue with God, saying an offering is an offering. The end justifies the means. If the outcome is the same, who cares how you get there? But God prescribes methods, not just outcomes. God does not just prescribe a harmonious home and family. He tells us what that means and how to achieve it. We are not free to redefine and reorganize God's plan. To go outside God's design is to dishonor Him. It is the very opposite of being "reverent in our behavior."

Not Malicious Gossips

Gossip is so common these days that it hardly registers on our sin radar. In fact, we might want to look at this phrase from Titus and say, "Well, I might gossip occasionally, but I am not a malicious gossip; so it must be all right." The fact is, in the Greek these are not two separate words ("malicious" and "gossips"). This is a single Greek word: *diabolos*. This word means "prone to slander, a false accuser, one who accuses or maligns." According to Vines dictionary, this word is used 34 times in the New Testament as a title for Satan. In fact, the English word "devil" comes from this exact word in the Greek. It means "accuser, slanderer."

Read Revelation 12:10.
What is Satan called in this verse?

What activity does Satan engage in day and night?

We know that when a person lies, they are speaking Satan's language (John 8:44). But do we realize that when we slander, accuse, and gossip we are also speaking Satan's language? We are actually being diabolical, according to Titus 2:3. That certainly sheds a new light on what has come to be a socially acceptable sin.

Gossip is Unloving

Satan is filled with hate, not love. Gossip is not fitting for an imitator of Christ because it is an unloving act.
Read 1 Corinthians 13:4-6.
In v.5, what is the last thing listed in this verse that love does NOT do?

When someone has wronged us in some way, the natural thing is to want to punish them for it, to make them suffer in return. One way we do that is by gossiping about the situation. We tell everyone who will listen so that we can lower the offender in the eyes of others. But according to this verse, love "does not take into account a wrong suffered." This is a Greek phrase that basically means not to take notice of something, not to consider it worth thinking about. For example, if you got a minor scratch on your arm and someone asked you what happened, you would probably say, "It's not even worth mentioning." That is the attitude implied by this phrase. A loving person takes so little notice of personal injury that they would never think of mentioning it to a third party.

What is the characteristic of love in v.6?

Another reason people gossip is out of the perverse delight in sharing a bit of scandal. Being the bearer of bad or shocking news carries a certain prestige with it. An unloving person will take delight in passing along the story of another's sin, disaster, or failure. Love would take no pleasure in repeating such a thing.

Both of these examples show us the best antidote to a gossiping tongue is a loving heart.

Gossip is Self-Exalting

Satan's original sin was the desire to exalt himself and to be like God (Is. 14:12-14). This is the exact opposite of Christ's self-abasing nature (Phil.2:7). As imitators of Christ, gossip is not fitting because it comes from the desire to lift myself up by putting another down.

Read Philippians 2:4.
What are we to look out for?

This mindset is incompatible with gossip.

Not Enslaved to Much Wine

We have already examined this characteristic as one that applies to every believer. Suffice it to say, Jesus had perfect balance in His physical appetites.

Read Luke 7:33-35.
What is Jesus (falsely) accused of being by the Pharisees in v.34?

John the Baptist was a particular kind of prophet who was held to a strict dietary standard that even Jesus did not live by. Jesus ate and drank in a way that was normal in the society of the day. Because of this, the religious leaders accused Him of being a glutton and drunkard. The strict diet of John seemed more fitting for a great and spiritual man of God than the things Jesus ate and drank, in the opinion of the Pharisees. But this was only because they had everything backwards, as usual.

Read Mark 7:14-23.
What is more important to a person's holiness – what they eat or what they say and do?

Read 1 Corinthians 10:31.
Is it possible to eat and drink in a way that brings glory to God?

Read Titus 1:12.
Is it possible to eat and drink in a way that does NOT bring glory to God?

The context in 1 Corinthians 10 explains that in matters such as eating and drinking, the important thing is that we keep a clear conscience before God and that we do everything – even things as seemingly insignificant as eating and drinking – in a way that glorifies Him and brings honor rather than dishonor to His gospel.

Not Mastered by Anything

In 1 Corinthians 6:12, Paul makes a clear statement about appetites:

"All things are lawful for me, but not all things are profitable. All things are lawful for me, but I will not be mastered by anything."

This is just another way of saying "not to be enslaved." We are not to allow anything to master us. We have already discussed this to some extent in the previous lesson when we looked at idols. But now we want to put this strictly in the context of food and drink.

In the very next verse, Paul writes, "Food is for the stomach and the stomach for food, but God will do away with them both." This means something similar to the modern saying, "Eat to live; don't live to eat."

Read Romans 14:17.
What is the kingdom of God NOT made up of?

What are the things of the kingdom?

Read Matthew 6:31-33.
What kinds of things do the people of the world ("Gentiles") focus all their mental energy upon?

What are we, as God's people, supposed to be preoccupied with?

Food has a tremendously disproportionate place in our thinking. A healthy interest in proper nutrition has given way to endless disorders and obsessions with food and eating. Issues surrounding food literally destroy many women's lives.

A wrongful obsession with food is not new. The worship of one's taste buds destroyed not just individuals but whole families as far back as Genesis. We are familiar with the messy, sometimes ugly, story of Jacob and Esau. We know of two brothers, rivals from birth, deceiving and avenging all their lives. But what we may not realize is that this all began with a father's obsession with food.

Read Genesis 25:27-28.
Why did Isaac favor his son Esau over Jacob?

Read Genesis 27:2-4.
What did Esau have to do before his father would give him his deathbed blessing?

Considering his father's bad example in his love of food, it is easy to see where Esau learned his own priorities. Read Genesis 25:29-33. What did Esau do?

An inordinate love of food is not a small sin. It is a deceitful and devastating form of bondage. We must recognize it as such and flee from it. The way to break free from enslavement to food is the same as what we learned regarding other idols. First identify and admit the hold that food has on you. Fasting from different kinds of foods can help you discover what you are enslaved by. Next call it what it is: sin. Confess it and repent of it. Finally, seek to replace your love for physical food with a love for spiritual food. Perhaps it would help to revisit *Right From the Start*, Lesson 3 on the care and feeding of the spiritual life. Determine to seek first the kingdom of God – not run after food and drink like the pagan world. Set your mind on the things above, the things of which the kingdom of God is made, not eating and drinking. Remember, the only way to displace one affection is with the "expulsive power of a new one."

Teach and Encourage the Younger Women

If someone were to ask you, "According to Titus 2:4, what are the older women to do to the younger women?" your answer would depend upon the Bible in your lap. If you held a King James Bible, you would answer *teach*. If you were reading in the New American Standard, you would say *encourage*. If you had a New International Version, you would find the word *train*. Why the discrepancy? What exactly are older women to do to younger women in God's design for discipleship? The fact is, none of these words is adequate in itself to answer that question. We need to embrace the meaning behind each one to get the whole picture.

The Greek etymology of the word in question in verse 4 makes it clear how each translator came up with a different English equivalent. The word "encourage" is *sophronizo*. It implies discipline and training in one's thinking. This word is derived from two others: *sozo*, which means to keep safe, protect, heal, make whole; and *phren*, which refers to sympathy, feelings, understanding, perception and judgment. This casserole of meanings presents us with a picture of how we are to help one another grow in Christ-likeness as women in our homes. There is a need for actual teaching – instruction from Scripture and practical help in applying its principles. There is also a need for sympathy and support through prayer or just being with someone during a time of difficulty. Finally, there is occasionally a need for tough words and strict accountability. Each of these approaches is wrapped up in that one word *encourage*.

Jesus modeled each approach in His dealings with His disciples. Consider these examples.

Read Mark 4:33-34.
Much of what Jesus taught the crowds went right over their heads. But what was Jesus doing privately with His disciples?

Read Matthew 16:23.
In this passage, Peter has just told Jesus that He will not have to die. Peter will protect Him and keep Him from going to the cross. Although Peter means well, Jesus gives Peter a sharp rebuke. What does He tell Peter?

Peter needed a quick correction because his perspective had shifted, for the moment, from God's Kingdom to a man's-kingdom way of thinking. Jesus stepped on this quickly before it could go any further.

Read Matthew 26:36-38.
What does Jesus want from His disciples, Peter and John, at this time of His greatest suffering?

Teach them to Love...

The method of the teaching includes instruction, correction, and support. The content of the teaching is love. Older women are to teach younger women to love their husbands and children. On the surface, this may seem unnecessary. After all, don't women naturally love their husbands and their children? Yes, actually, they do. They love them **naturally**. They do not love them **spiritually**. The kind of love that comes natural to us as women is not the kind of love Jesus exhibited. Our love can be possessive, envious, smothering, manipulative, and selfish. Jesus' love was none of these.

Right From the Start, Lesson Four was entitled, "The One Commandment." In that lesson, we studied the kind of love that is a fruit of the Spirit of God, the product of abiding in Christ. We will not duplicate that material here. Go back and review that lesson if you are able, and this time apply it directly to your relationships in the home. Look at 1 Corinthians 13:4-8 as a wife and a mother. Are you patient and kind? Or are you jealous, boastful, and arrogant? Do you seek your own way? Are you easily provoked? Do you keep score meticulously, never forgetting a wrong done to you? Or do you bear all things patiently? It doesn't take long for us to realize how far we fall short of Christ's standard for love.

Another kind of love

The Greek word for love in 1 Corinthians 13 is *agape*. This kind of love is a characteristic of God, and it is a fruit of the Spirit in the believer's life (Galatians 5:22). But interestingly, that is not the Greek word used in Titus 2:4. The word used in this passage is *philandros*. It is a compound word made up of the word *philos*, meaning "a friend, companion" and *andros* meaning (in this context) "husband." The word is an adjective, not a verb. It describes the wife's nature, not just her actions. It literally means she is to be a "husband-loving" woman. The woman is also to have this kind of love for her children. She is also to be *philoteknos* – a child-lover.

This is not just a matter of semantics. There is a big difference between doing the duties of wife and mother and being a woman who loves her family in this way. This kind of woman would find her deepest needs for friendship and companionship met within her family. She would not need a weekly "girls night out" or "mom's day out" to get away from her husband and kids. She would enjoy being with them – not begrudge serving them.

This is a counter-cultural idea. Our society tells women they need to have something just for themselves. They need "me time" to get back a bit of what they have poured out all week. But remember, Jesus is our model. Can you imagine Him needing "me time"? He needed time alone with His Father for prayer, but He did not have one single thing in His life that was just for Himself. Yet He called His disciples "friends" (John 15:15). He loved them – not with the love of duty but with affection.

It is so easy for a wife to fall into a dutiful, heartless kind of love. We can feel like we do more than our part because of all our acts of service to our husbands and children. But that is not *phileo* love. It is not what our families need from us.

One song in the musical *Fiddler on the Roof* illustrates this perfectly. Golde and her husband Tevye are a middle-aged Orthodox Jewish couple in Russia. True to their culture, they had an arranged marriage when they were very young. Tevye knew that his wife had to marry him, whether she loved him or not. But that is not enough for him anymore. He needs to know if she has any real affection for him. The song begins with Tevye posing the question, "Do you love me?" Golde tries to evade him for a while, then finally answers:

Do I love you?
For twenty-five years I've washed your clothes
Cooked your meals, cleaned your house
Given you children, milked the cow
After twenty-five years, why talk about love right now?

He continues to press her for a confession of real love. Finally she gives in, with an awkward, "Well I suppose I do." He is delighted and replies, "Then I suppose I love you, too."

This is a lighthearted way to express a very real need. God Himself is not even satisfied with dutiful acts with no heart in them.

Read Isaiah 29:13.
What is God's complaint?

Read Mark 7:5-6.
Who does Jesus accuse of this same sin?

Old Testament or New, God does not want people to love Him with acts of duty alone devoid of any heart. The greatest commandment is to "love the Lord" – not just serve Him. He wants fervent hearts, not just words or deeds.

Read Revelation 2:1-5.
Remember, Ephesians 5 compares our relationship with Jesus to a marriage. In this passage, Jesus commends his Bride in Ephesus for perseverance, faithful service, and dedication to the truth. But He has one complaint. What is it?

Jesus, as Husband to the Church, wants fervent affection. He is not content with a dutiful Bride. He wants her heart as well. If Jesus seeks this from His Bride, the Church, it is right and fitting that our own husbands would seek it from us.

All of us need one another's help to grow in this kind of love. We need to be taught what this love looks like in action. We need to be corrected when an unloving attitude takes hold. And, finally, we need to be supported when our attempts to love cause us great pain and disappointment. At these times, we need one another to be there to "watch and pray" with us. No single aspect of teaching is sufficient. Each of us needs all three. These three together make up the heart of the Titus 2 command, "Teach them to love…"

…To be Sensible

We have spent a great deal of time on being sensible in a previous lesson. I just want to add one thought to what we have already learned about this word.

Years ago I heard Elisabeth Elliot speak. It was a great privilege to see her in person. She was impressive in every way. She had an aura of strength and dignity about her that you could actually feel. She was addressing women, and the title of her message was "Equanimity." She was speaking about moodiness and emotional unpredictability and how women often excuse these things in themselves as part of being feminine. At one point, she paused and looked directly at us and said, "Just how nasty do you think you have the right to be?" The words themselves were not particularly profound; but the combination of the simple truth and the weightiness of the personal example set by that particular woman's life burned those words into my memory. To this day I cannot have a "mood swing" without them coming back to haunt me.

Sensibility is much like equanimity. It is not simply a matter of being rational rather than emotional. It is being reasonable rather than unreasonable, and I believe it is a quality that needs to be modeled as well as taught.

... To Be Pure

As Christians, we should be characterized by purity, modesty, and innocence. In the culture we live in, we should stand apart like blazing beacons of light against a pitch black sky (Phil. 2:15).

Read 1Thess. 4:3-8.
What is God's will (v.3)?

What has God called us to (v.7)?

According to v.5, from whom are we to be different?

What are those who don't know God driven by (v.5)?

Verse 4 is the heart of this passage. It says that each one of us needs to learn how to possess our own vessel in sanctification and honor. This verse gives us the reason and the motivation for our purity of life.

To **possess**, in the Greek, means, "to acquire, get, or procure a thing for one's self, to possess." It is interesting that we are told to actively acquire and possess our bodies. We would assume that we already possess them. But this command implies that perhaps we do not have our bodies in our possession the way we are intended to.

Consider Romans 6:12-13.
What are we told NOT to do with our bodies?

If we offer our bodies as instruments of sin, we are not possessing our vessels. We are giving them away. In Romans 6, the word for "instrument" means a weapon of war. Offering our bodies to sin is equated to arming the enemy. It is treason against God. A different word is used to describe our bodies in 1 Thessalonians. The word **vessel** means an implement, like a household utensil. It implies an object designed for a particular use. We are to possess our bodies like we would keep sharp knives or well-oiled machines in our houses. We are to keep them for their proper use and not give them away to be used improperly.

We are to keep our bodies in a state of **sanctification**. This, too, implies something set apart for its good and proper use. We are to keep our bodies reserved for those activities which please God, not use them in a way that is displeasing.

The word translated **honor** in 1 Thessalonians 4:4 speaks of the value by which a price is fixed. This means that the value of our bodies is determined by the price paid to acquire them.

Read 1 Corinthians 6:20.
Why should we glorify God in our bodies?

Now read 1 Peter 1:18-19.
What was the purchase price for our bodies?

Read Proverbs 6:26.
What does immorality do to the value (or "honor") of a human being?

When we give ourselves to immorality, we are selling our bodies at the price of bread – the very same bodies that were paid for with the precious blood of Christ. This certainly puts things in perspective for us.

Impurity Illustrated

There are many ways impurity rears its ugly head. Some are obvious (like premarital or extramarital sex), but others are more subtle. It is important that we evaluate our behavior honestly so we are sure that we call sin all that God calls sin. Our society is so tainted with moral filth that we can easily believe we are innocent because we are using the world as a benchmark for comparison. But the world is not our standard; we measure ourselves against a holy God. He is the one we are to please.

In thought or imagination

According to Matthew 5:27-28, does God make a distinction between sexual sin done in the body and sexual sin done in the mind?

This verse targets men, but the same is true for women. Any kind of fantasy or imagination of immorality is just as sinful as the act itself.

Another thing to consider under this category is our entertainment. Romans 1:32 speaks of the guilt of people who enjoy and applaud the sinful acts of others. Can we justify being entertained by immorality in the media? Are we open to letting God speak to us in this area?

In appearance

Read Proverbs 7:10.
How is the woman in this passage dressed?

According to v.19, this woman is not a prostitute. She is a married woman, but she dresses like a prostitute.

Read 1 Peter 3:3-4.
What should NOT be the source of a woman's beauty?

What SHOULD be the source of her beauty?

Read 1 Timothy 2:9-10.
How are women NOT to dress?

Paul uses the words "modesty, decency, and good sense" to describe how women are to dress. His intention is clear: women are not to draw attention to themselves by their clothing. This does not mean they have to be drab and covered from head to toe. One could argue that such an extreme attracts as much attention to the woman as immodest or overly-flashy clothing would. Paul is calling for decency and good taste. He is saying that the woman's character and good deeds should be more memorable than her outfits.

Read Revelation 3:17.
What does this person think their condition is?

What is their actual condition?

This verse perfectly describes women who focus exclusively on their outer beauty, but give no thought to the condition of the inner person of their heart. In a culture that idolizes the physical, Jesus calls us to focus primarily on the spiritual. This is the way of His kingdom, and it should be the perspective of His people.

Read 1 Thess. 5:22-23.
Many translations render verse 22, "Abstain from every form of evil." The King James translated it, "Abstain from every appearance of evil." That is actually a better word choice. The Greek word used here means, "external or outward appearance, form or shape." If it looks evil, we should steer clear of it.

I don't know how often we apply this to our clothing, but it would be wise to do so. Verse 23 establishes the context of the warning: the sanctification of our spirit, soul, and body. If we are to be holy and pure through and through, we must also look the part outwardly.

Sometimes we downplay appearances too much as an over-reaction against hypocrisy. We all know that high necklines and long skirts do not guarantee there is a pure heart beating underneath the outfit. But wouldn't it seem that a pure heart might have some bearing on necklines and hemlines? It is worth thinking about.

Purity Encapsulated

It is important to remember, the Christian life is all about principles – not laws. We are not given specific instructions outlining how we should relate to the opposite sex in every possibly situation. But neither are we left to our own devises. We have two things to help us. We have the Word of God, which contains guiding principles for every issue of life; and we have the Holy Spirit Who personalizes and applies those principles to us moment by moment each day.

Read 1 Timothy 5:1-2.
Note at the end of verse 2, Paul's concern is Timothy's purity.
How is he to relate to older women? What is his guiding principle?

How is he to relate to younger women? What is his guiding principle?

Paul was speaking of men and women within the church, but the same principles could be applied in any context. If we were to take this to heart, we would find practical applications emerge quite readily. Consider these examples:

- Suppose I am a woman who works in an office. My boss is an older man. When I get dressed in the morning, I am going to think of that boss as if he were my father. I am not going to dress with the intent to stir any response in that man that I would not want to stir in my own father.

- Suppose I am a mom who goes to a play group for parents of toddlers at the YMCA. There is a mixture of moms and dads, all roughly my age, who meet there weekly with their children. The parents chat while the kids play games. I am going to relate to the men in the group as if they were my brothers. I am not going to flirt or foster any dynamic in conversation with them that I would not foster with my own brother.

In every situation, I am going to take the principle of Scripture and I am going to let the Holy Spirit guide me in applying it with wisdom and discretion in my daily activities and relationships.

Workers at Home

The phrase translated "workers at home" in Titus 2:5 is actually just one Greek word, *oikourgos*. This word is derived from two others: *oikos*, meaning a house or a household, and *ouros*, meaning a keeper or a guard. When we think of the word "housekeeper," we probably picture a matronly woman with a starched apron and cap and a ring of keys on her belt who bosses around the other servants. This image has much more to do with a Charles Dickens novel than it does with Christian womanhood.

The part of the word that means "keeper" can also be used of a door keeper or a gate keeper. The idea is that the woman is a watcher over her home. This involves both her presence in her home and her mindset toward her home. She must be there, at her post so to speak. She must also realize what her responsibility is.

The woman's role in the home can be compared to Jesus' role as the "door of the sheep."

Read John 10:1-11.
In verse 3, who decides whether someone is let into the sheep fold or not?

In verse 7, who is not only the doorkeeper, but the door?

Who or what is Jesus trying to keep out (v.1, 10)?

As the keeper of the house, all of the comings and goings of the family must pass through the wife/mother. Like the faithful shepherd, she has a role of both protection and management. As a protector, nothing gets in unless it gets by her first. Anything that would bring danger or destruction to her family is stopped at the door. As a manager, she "looks well to the ways of her household" (Prov.31:27), seeing to it that everyone has what they need.

Protection

When I speak of the mother's role of protection in the home, obviously by this I do not mean protection against physical intruders. The woman's strength is to be found in her wisdom and discernment (Prov.31:25-26). The mother has a responsibility to guard the hearts and minds of her family, keeping out evil influences that would damage them spiritually. Just as the Good Shepherd guarded His flock from false teachers, being the Doorkeeper that kept them out, the woman, as a keeper in her home, guards her little flock with wisdom, discernment, and faithful instruction (Prov.31:26).

Some may argue that this is the husband's responsibility. Ultimately, it is. But we can't sidestep the meaning of this word in Titus 2. We do have an important role to play. Generally speaking, the mother is the one who is present in the home more hours of the day than the father. She is the one who has the time and opportunity to stay on top of what comes into the house by way of iPods, computers, game systems, books, friends, etc. She can perform the helpful role of information gathering, assessing and analyzing these things, then bring them to her husband for his final verdict. This is something wives should discuss with their husbands, asking them what role they want to play themselves and what parts of this task they wish to delegate to their wives.

As mothers, we cannot shirk this responsibility. We need to examine ourselves: Are we careless or lazy about this task? Do we pass it off on our husbands, even though we know that they do not have the time or the constant access to our children's lives that we do? If so, we need to repent and resume our post.

Management

The wife's role as "keeper of her home" also includes a management component. Countless volumes have been written on this subject, but none more concise than the single chapter of Proverbs 31. Take a moment to read Proverbs 31:10-31. Read it carefully, but try not to get hung up on each detail. Rather, let the chapter form a general picture in your mind of the kind of woman God wants us to be.

Many women find this passage to be very oppressive. They feel judged or hopeless the minute they read it. They see it as a call to an impossible ideal. But that is why we need to look at it for what it is: a portrait of a kind of woman – not a law or a curriculum to follow to the letter. We need to glean principles from it, not place ourselves under an unnecessary burden.

Before we look at these principles, I want to make one more defense of this proverb. If we were honest, we'd have to admit that contemporary culture places a far heavier burden of expectation on women than this Proverb ever did. Each era crafts for itself an image of the "ideal" woman. In the past women have been idealized in every extreme -- from being ultra-feminine, swooning weaklings forbidden to have an intellect to being tough, masculine, and aggressive with no feminine characteristics whatsoever. In our current day, women are expected to be funny, smart, and attractive (even "sexy") at any age. They are expected to work, stay at home with the kids, and join the gym – all at the same time. They are expected to have gorgeous homes, stylish wardrobes, and talented children. Women are harshly judged on outward appearances. The priority is on looking good and making an impression on other women.

Against that backdrop, I think we will find it is actually a relief to look at the clarity and simplicity of the kind of woman that is esteemed in God's Word. In contrast to the American ideal, the Proverbs woman is down to earth and accessible. She is natural and lovely.

We are just going to look at her basic qualities. How they flesh out day to day will vary from household to household, just as it varies from century to century. It is up to the Holy Spirit, your conscience, and your husband to help you bring the following principles into specific focus for your own application.

Use the following points (taken in order from Proverbs 31:10-31) for careful self-assessment. Evaluate yourself in these areas and then prayerfully consider where you could change and improve. Don't neglect to thank God that His ideal is not impossible, like the world's. His commands are not burdensome (1 John 5:3).

- Capable – She knows how to accomplish what needs to be done. She has learned the skills necessary to good homemaking (cooking, cleaning, mending, laundering, etc.).

- Trustworthy – Her husband can delegate things to her, knowing they will be properly taken care of.

- Hard working – She works with willing hands. She doesn't begrudge her housework. She is not lazy.

- Meal preparation – She plans ahead and shops and cooks meals for her family.

- Shopping – She shops carefully, within her budget, with an eye to quality and thrift.

- Money management – She is aware of wise and foolish investments. She does not waste money or make foolish purchases.

- Hospitality/Generosity – She gives to the poor and cares for the needs of others.

- Confident – She is not anxiety-ridden. She does not fear the future because she plans ahead carefully and trusts in the Lord.

- Good reputation – Not only does she have a good reputation, but she reflects well on her husband and brings him honor. She does not outshine him.

- Wisdom and instruction – She knows God's Word and can offer good advice to her husband when asked and to her children as she diligently instructs them in the ways of God.

- Watchful – She watches over the activities of her household. She oversees everyone's schedules and routines. She keeps things running smoothly.

- Her husband and children praise her – It is one thing to be praised by outsiders, but to be praised by your family means you are the genuine article – the same good, wise, loving person at home as out in public. A hypocrite is never praised by her own family!

- Inner Beauty – This woman does not prioritize physical beauty. She understands that such beauty is fleeting, temporary, and earthly. Inner beauty is lasting – and it is what God esteems (1 Peter 3:3-4).

On the one hand, this is quite a description. But on the other hand, it is so compatible with all the other characteristics of godliness that we have been studying, we can expect to improve as wives and homemakers as we grow in other areas of Christlikeness.

...To Be Kind

Kindness is a simple word and an unassuming virtue; it is easy to overlook. But kindness is the very heartbeat of the gospel.

Read Luke 6:35.
Who is kind, and to whom?

Read Romans 2:4.
What leads us to repentance and salvation?

Read 1 Peter 2:3.
If we are believers, what have we tasted?

Read Ephesians 4:32.
What are we to be?

To whom?

Why (on what basis)?

There is another place that this word appears, but it is hidden beneath a different English translation.

Read Matthew 11:30.

The word translated "easy" is the same Greek word for "kind" found in the other verses above. This verse could be rendered, "My yoke is kindly and my burden is light." Jesus is saying that the very life of discipleship He calls us to, difficult as it is, is a kindness to us. The life of a follower and imitator of Christ is the only truly good life. For that reason, it is kind.

Jesus did many things out of sheer kindness. Let's consider just two examples.

Read Luke 7:12-15.
Why was this man's death a particular tragedy, according to v.12?

What did Jesus do in v.15?

Read Matthew 15:32-37.
Why didn't Jesus want to send the people away as they were?

What did He do?

If we are to be imitators of Christ, we need to follow His example in doing acts of kindness.
Read Matthew 25:31-46.
What is the basis for proving which people were truly Jesus' followers and which were imposters?

Jesus says the righteous will ask, "Lord, when did we see You hungry, and feed You, or thirsty, and give You *something* to drink?" and Jesus answers, "Truly I say to you, to the extent that you did it to one of these brothers of Mine, *even* the least *of them*, you did it to Me."

When I had my first four children, and they were all under the age of eight, I felt overwhelmed by their constant demands. Then one day, the Lord showed me this passage in a new light. To remind myself of my lesson, I bought a plain white apron. On it, I drew four little stick figures to represent my children. I drew little word bubbles above their heads, which said, "Feed me!" "Dress me!" "Give me a drink!" Across the bottom of the apron I wrote, "When you did it unto one of the least of these, you did it unto Me!" That changed my perspective on these little people who needed so much from me at that stage of their lives. Suddenly these many acts of kindness being wrung out of me day and night took on an eternal weight of glory.

Being Submissive to Their Own Husbands

We have already looked at submission twice in this study. We have seen that it is one of the defining characteristics of Christ. When He calls each of us to imitate Him, He is calling us to a life of submission. For the woman, this shows up primarily in her home. As Jesus submitted gladly to the Father, wives are to submit gladly to their husbands.

Read Ephesians 5:22.
How is the wife to submit to her husband?

Read Titus 2:5.
Why is the wife to submit to her husband?

When we submit to our husbands, we are really submitting to the Lord. We yield to Him when we yield to our husbands. And we do it so that God's Word will not be dishonored.

Read 1 Peter 3:1-2.
According to v.1, if a woman's husband is an unbeliever (or perhaps a disobedient believer), what can she do to win him over to the Lord?

There is power in submission because submission proves the truth of the gospel. It is so natural to bully and manipulate one's husband, that when a woman instead is respectful and submissive it bears weighty testimony to the truth of the gospel message. There is no other explanation for such behavior. Just as Jesus' miracles made many people say, "Surely this man comes from God," the miracle of a submissive spirit causes people to say, "Surely this woman has encountered Christ."

Conclusion

In this lesson, we have seen more specifically what Christ would look like if He were displayed fully by a woman in her home. It is important to remember, we do NOT become like Christ by striving in our own strength and wisdom to copy His actions; but rather, we become like Him by gazing upon Him, studying Him, soaking in His Words and His life through the gospels, praying to Him constantly and walking with Him daily. The branch that abides in the vine bears the fruit of the Spirit. The soul that fixes its gaze on Christ as in a mirror comes to match Christ's reflection there. Spend much time with Him, and you will grow to be like Him from the inside out.

Matters for Prayer

This lesson addresses many "departments" of our lives as women, wives, and mothers.

Take the time to review this lesson carefully in the weeks to come. Pray over one section a day, with a notebook in hand, and ask the Holy Spirit to convict, instruct, and guide you in recognizing sin, repenting of it, and making real changes. Write down what He reveals to you. It is so easy to forget and let lessons and convictions slip away.

You may want to share the areas of conviction with a mature sister in Christ so she can pray with you and for you, as well as keep you accountable for change.

Remember, a change in behavior without an accompanying change of heart does not create Christ; it creates a Pharisee (Matthew 23:25-26). Only God can change your heart. Ask Him to cleanse you from the inside out. Labor in prayer, like Paul did, asking the Father daily to form Christ in you (Gal.4:19).

Lesson Seven

Christ's Reflection in the Workplace

In Lesson Six, we focused on what the book of Titus has to say about women living out Christ's example in the context of their homes. We learned that the Christ-like woman is devoted to the Lord, like an Old Testament priest in the temple. Every act she does is consecrated to God. No act is insignificant when carried out with this understanding. We learned that she is not to be a malicious gossip because gossip is, according to the Greek, diabolical in nature. It is Satan's own language, and it is suitable to Satan's nature (unloving and self-exalting), not Christ's. The Christ-like woman is also self-controlled in her appetites, eating and drinking in a way that brings glory to God. We saw that the older women are to both teach and encourage the younger women in their growth in Christ. Finally, we looked at the content which that teaching is supposed to include.

In this lesson we are going to shift our gaze to the qualities of "workers." Even though some of what we are going to be looking at was written to men in its original context, this lesson is also applicable to women because, as we have said before, Christ's character is consistent. He is a perfect example to all of us. The characteristics and attitudes that make up a God-honoring worker are the same for women as they are for men. They apply both within the home and outside of it. These verses also give those of us who are mothers some guidelines regarding what character qualities are important to instill in our sons.

Jesus in the Workplace

"Older men are to be temperate, dignified, sensible, sound in faith, in love, in perseverance ... Likewise urge the young men to be sensible... Urge bondslaves to be subject to their own masters, in everything, to be well-pleasing, not argumentative, not pilfering, but showing all good faith that they may adorn the doctrine of God our Savior in every respect." (Titus 2:2, 6, 9-10)

In Lesson Five we studied what it means to be temperate, sensible, and sound; so we are going to skip over those traits in this lesson. We will begin our study with the command to be dignified.

Dignified

When we think of dignity, we probably conjure up a rather stuffy image. In my mind, at least, dignity connotes a stern old man with an aristocratic bearing. But the actual meaning of this word is much more practical. The Greek word is *semnos*, and it means venerable, grave, honorable, honest. It is a derivative of the word that means "gravity." Let's pause for a moment and consider the idea of gravity.

In the late 1800s a Christian writer named George MacDonald published a short story called "The Light Princess." This was a fairy tale about a princess who was born with no gravity. In a brilliant use of symbolism and double meanings, MacDonald created a character who was both lighter than air (having no gravity in the sense of her physical weight) and also was so lighthearted of disposition that she could not cry (having no gravity in the sense of substance to her character). She laughed at everything and could take nothing seriously. She was a source of grief to her parents, both in their constant fear that she would float over the castle wall and be lost forever, and in their worry that she could never become a good queen, since she had no serious side to her nature. A person who lacks the kind of dignity Paul is writing about in Titus is like the Light Princess. He might be the life of the party, so to speak; but he would not be a person you could approach in any kind of crisis. He would be fun for a laugh but of no use if you were suffering or had a serious need.

Aristotle defined the Greek word *semnos* as a balance "between not caring if you please anyone and endeavoring at all costs to please everyone." Dignity means having a level of social decorum that is pleasant to be around. It is on the one hand not crude, loud, obnoxious, insincere, or constantly jovial. On the other hand, it is not groveling and overly deferential.

Once again, Jesus is our model.

According to Isaiah 42:2, what did Jesus NOT do?

In Isaiah 53:2 we are told, "He has no stately form or majesty that we should look upon Him, nor appearance that we should be attracted to Him." Jesus did not draw attention to Himself with an impressive appearance or a domineering personality. But, as we see throughout the gospels, He was not a wallflower either. He engaged people, taught in the synagogues, and interacted with crowds. All His dealings with men were frank, honest, open, and sincere. They were not flashy and showy, but also not invisible (Matt.26:55). This is the kind of balance the word *dignified* implies.

We need to evaluate ourselves. Are we dignified? Do we have an appropriate amount of gravity to our character? Do people know that there is something of substance to us — that they can talk seriously to us and we will be able to relate? Do people see us as flighty? Shallow? Is the impression that we give of ourselves accurate, or is there another side to us that we tend to hide? If our goal in relating to people is deeper than just to be popular and well-liked socially, we will realize that we don't do ourselves or others any favors by hiding our serious side.

Subject to their Masters

The culture in which Paul wrote the book of Titus was one where slavery was common. Much of the workforce in the Roman Empire was made up of slaves. This was an accepted part of the economy, and Paul writes within this context. We must set that cultural distinction aside and apply the principles behind these commands to employees and employers in the workplace.

As we have said elsewhere in this study, submission is for everyone. When we take up Christ's yoke, it is a yoke of gentleness and humility worn with a heart of submission. This is exactly the mindset that a Christian worker is expected to have toward his employer. Submission, as we learned in a previous lesson, means to "arrange under." A submissive employee places himself willingly under the authority of his boss and accepts that his role is to please his boss in every respect.

American society is antagonistic to this attitude. Our economy is one of free enterprise. In recent decades there has been an explosion of small businesses. Everyone wants to be their own boss. Much of what drives this is a desire not to be under authority. It is common these days to hear people say things like, "I just can't work for so-and-so," or, "He can't tell me what to do," or, "I won't be treated like that!" This attitude is the opposite of Christ's. He submitted Himself to a sinful government and allowed Himself to be judged by wicked men. Not only that, but He lived every moment of every day not as an autonomous, self-made Man, but as an obedient Son to His Father.

Whose message did Jesus teach? (John 7:16)

Whose glory did Jesus seek? (John 7:17-18)

Whose initiative does Jesus act upon? (John 8:28)

Who does Jesus aim to please with His actions? (John 8:29)

Whose will governed Jesus' actions? (Matt. 26:39)

If anyone had a right to be "self-employed" it was Jesus. But He did not exercise any of His rights. Instead He took upon Himself the position of a mere slave and lived a life entirely characterized by obedience to Another – even to the point of death (Phil. 2:7-8). And yet He did so, not with resentment but with joy (Heb. 12:2).

Well-Pleasing

Not only is the worker to be submissive to his employer, he is to be well-pleasing to him as well. In most of the places where this word is used in the New Testament, the context refers to a believer being well-pleasing to the Lord.

Read Romans 12:1-2.
Once the believer has presented himself to God, what will he be able to discern?

Read 2 Corinthians 5:9.
What should be our ambition?

Read Ephesians 5:8-10.
What are we to try to learn?

Notice in these verses, we are to try to find out what is pleasing to God – and then do it.
The Christian worker should serve his employer in the very same way that he serves the Lord (Col. 3:23-24). He should find out what pleases his employer and then do it.

A Point of Application

This attitude should also be applied by wives in their housework. We should find out what pleases our husbands – what is important to them. Do they like a clean kitchen? Decluttered surfaces? Organized household papers? What is important to them should be important to us. If we were working in an office, we would not think of managing everything our own way with flagrant disregard for how our boss wanted things done. We should not do this in our homes either. We should find out what pleases our husbands in the managing of our homes – and then do it.

Not Argumentative

To be argumentative means to speak against, to contradict, to oppose, to decline to obey. The Christ-like employee will not do these things to his employer. He will very simply do what he is told without complaining.

Read Philippians 2:14-15.
According to v.14, what are we NOT to do?

What reason is given for this in v.15?

These words shed some helpful light on the Titus 2 passage. Not only are we not to outwardly argue with our employers when they give us a task to do, but we are not even to do so inwardly. The Greek word for *grumble* in Phil. 2:14 means, "a secret debate or displeasure not openly avowed." This implies not only an attitude that is resistant to being told what to do, but it also implies an element of hypocrisy. It implies that a person might comply with his boss' demands outwardly yet still be stirring up dissent behind the scenes – perhaps just in his own mind or even among other employees.

Philippians 2:15 gives us the reason we are to do all things without grumbling or complaining. If we do not complain, we will shine like stars among ordinary men. Complaining is a hallmark of human nature. Whenever a person feels inconvenienced, put out, uncomfortable, or bothered in any way, he naturally complains about it. Anyone who has ever had a job knows this is true. I would not dare to venture a percentage, but I would guess that the majority of the communication among co-workers in the workplace includes an element of complaining, whether overtly stated or just implied. Not only this, but when a man (or woman) comes home from work, sits down to dinner, and talks about their day, much of what comes forth is complaining.

The worker who has embraced his job as another arena where he can imitate Christ will not behave this way. He will do his work heartily as to the Lord, without arguing, without complaining. In so doing, he will shine brightly for Christ. His attitude and conduct will be irrefutable evidence that the gospel is true. Likewise, the wife who has embraced her responsibility to manage her house "as unto the Lord" will not grumble and complain (inwardly or outwardly) about the jobs she has to do.

Not Pilfering

To pilfer is "to keep back something that belongs to another." An obvious application of this would be stealing money or products from your workplace; but perhaps a much more common (and overlooked) application would be that of pilfering time.

In his masterpiece *Screwtape Letters*, C.S. Lewis writes from the perspective of a senior devil teaching a junior devil how to undermine the Christian faith of a new believer. Screwtape encourages his apprentice to capitalize on the young man's perspective on time. He explains that humans wake up each morning considering themselves to be the rightful owners of a 24 hour day. Because they have this attitude toward time, they feel a certain level of resentment when that time is taken from them or they are not free to spend it as they please. This shows up in various areas, including their attitude toward their work.

When we are born of God, we should understand that our new life has come from Him. He has purchased us with the precious blood of Christ (1 Peter 1:19) and we belong to Him (1 Cor. 6:20). Therefore, when we wake up in the morning, we are not the *owners* of a 24 hour day. Rather, we are the *stewards* of a 24 hour day. Our time is God's and we are to spend it as He dictates. That includes doing all our work heartily and for His glory while at our jobs.

Read Ephesians 6:6.
How are we to work?

Whom are we to please?

Read Colossians 3:22.
How are we to work?

Read Luke 17:7-10.
In today's workforce, many people seem to feel that they should be recognized, thanked, and rewarded for simply doing the job they were hired and paid to do. Many companies have incentives and bonuses in place to encourage their workers to be on time and not to call in sick. How does Jesus address this attitude? What does He say a worker has a "right" to expect?

According to v.10, should a worker feel virtuous and praiseworthy for simply doing their job?

If Christian employees today were willing to adopt the attitude of a faithful slave, they would be closer to accurately following Jesus' example. We should come to work each day as if our employer owned us for those eight hours, seeing our time as belonging to him or her – not us. Then we would have God's perspective on wasting time, taking a long lunch, leaving early, or answering personal email on the job. We would see that those things are a type of pilfering, holding back from our employers what is rightfully theirs.

Showing Good Faith

To show good faith in one's work is to be trustworthy and faithful. It means to do your best for your employer whether he is watching you or not. If you have ever read the gospels, you will remember that Jesus told many stories that had to do with a master going away and leaving workers in charge of his business during his absence. The faithfulness of the servant was always proved (or disproved) during the master's absence.

Read Matthew 24:45-51.
What kind of servant is "blessed" by God (v.46)?

What did the wicked slave do when his master did not return for a long time?

Now read Matthew 25:19-21.
This is the middle of a longer parable. Basically, a master has left three servants in charge of investing his property in his absence.
What did the slave do when his master was away (v.20)?

What did the master think about the job the slave had done (v.21)?

If your faithfulness in your work is based on who is physically watching you, then you are not working for the Lord -- because He is always watching!

Read Matthew 6:1.
What are we to beware of doing?

The implication of this verse (and the teaching of the verses that follow) is that we are to do all things to be seen by God, not by men. If we are dependent on the praise of men to do our work, we are not faithful servants of the Lord. We should do our work consistently in good faith because it is the Lord that we serve.

Why It Matters

Read Titus 2:10.
What is the effect of a worker who is pleasing, not argumentative, not pilfering, and showing good faith? What does it accomplish?

We want to adorn the gospel of God. We want to make it beautiful and appealing. We want to prove it true by the way we live. This brings God glory and lifts up Christ. This proves that the gospel is powerful and effective. Our Christianity must show up in the most basic areas of life – like what time we arrive at work in the morning, how we talk to our co-workers, and how hard we work when the boss is out of the building. Remember, Christianity is not a set of beliefs that we hold in our head or a set of rules we follow by sheer willpower. Christianity is an entire way of living and being that comes from the inside out. It will define every single thing we do.

We are citizens of the Kingdom of God, not the kingdom of this world. This world's kingdom has clearly defined negative attitudes toward work. Our attitudes should be the exact opposite of these. When we perform our jobs in the way we have studied in this lesson, we will stand out as different. This will give us credibility as we share Christ with others.

Matters for Prayer

Confess to the Lord any sin or selfishness in your attitude toward your work. Ask Him to help you see your work His way.

Ask God to change your perspective on time — to see yourself as a steward rather than an owner of the 24 hours you are entrusted with each day. Ask Him to help you willingly accept that when you are at work, your time is the property of your employer.

Pray that you will come to see your job as service to the Lord, not to men. Ask God to help you find joy, contentment, and satisfaction in your work, knowing it is the Lord Whom you serve.

Ask the Holy Spirit to convict you immediately every time you complain. Cooperate with Him as He re-trains you in this area.

Pray that the gospel will be adorned by the way you conduct yourself each day — whether at home or on the job — so God will be glorified, Jesus will be lifted up, and the Word of God will be vindicated by your actions.

Parents- start praying now for your sons particularly to have this attitude toward work. Pray that they will see it as a joy, not a burden, and as valuable service to the Lord.

Lesson Eight

The Titus Model: A Ministry of Example

By now the book of Titus should be fairly familiar to you. But, in preparation for this lesson, take a few minutes to quickly read it over again, in its entirety.

So far, we have been discussing the importance of our behavior as Christians in the context of reflecting well upon the gospel message. We have learned that the outside world will judge the truth and value of the gospel by how we live our lives. By our conduct, we either adorn or dishonor the message we carry.

But the book of Titus gives us a second reason to pay close attention to our conduct. The unbelievers outside the church are not the only ones watching us; the younger believers inside are watching as well. Paul places high priority on the need for church leaders and men and women who are older in the faith to set a good example for younger, newer Christians.

For example, read Titus 2:3-5.
In verse 3, older women are commanded to behave a certain way. But notice the sentence does not end with verse 3. The thought continues straight on into verse 4. Older women are to be all these things "so that" they can teach younger women to be what they need to be.

Read Titus 2:6-8.
What does Paul tell Titus himself to be in v.7?

God's design for growth in the Christian life is very personal, very one-on-one. He even used this model Himself when He became a human being and walked the earth. Jesus could have lived a hermit's life, holding office hours for healing. He could have written His own gospels on a nice set of matching scrolls. He could have died, been raised again, and then passed His scrolls on to a faithful scribe and returned to heaven. Jesus could have done it this way if all He had to impart was a message. But Jesus did not only come to die for us. He came to live for us, to give us an example to follow and footsteps to walk in. Jesus' entire legacy comes to us through the men He lived with day and night during his three ministry years. As He taught them and lived in front of them, they became like Him -- imperfectly at first but increasingly more so over time. Jesus chose the model of personal discipleship as His means of initiating the Christian faith. According to the rest of the New Testament, He never intended for that model to change.

Jesus' Last Words

When Jesus returned to Heaven, He left His people with a command that is often referred to as "The Great Commission."

Read Matthew 28:18-20.
What does Jesus say that we are to "make" in v.19?

Making disciples is not the same as making converts. To make a convert means to get someone to agree to a creed by signing a card or adopting a list of doctrines. But as we learned many lessons ago, Christianity is not a creed. It is a Spirit-born life. Making disciples is like spiritual parenting. To make disciples means to take Spiritual newborns and teach and train them deliberately until they reach maturity. This is done partly by words but mostly by example.

Paul's Example

No one mirrors the heart of Christ for making disciples quite like Paul does.

Read 1 Thess. 2:8.
What TWO things did Paul impart to the Thessalonian Christians?

Look at 1 Thess. 2:7.
How does Paul describe his ministry among the new believers in Thessalonica?

Read 1 Corinthians 4:14-17.
What does Paul call these believers in v.14?

The Corinthians were fond of impressive Bible teachers, but Paul reminds them that teachers are a dime a dozen. Fathers, on the other hand are not. He is not just another teacher to them; he is their spiritual father (v.15). He is a father to them partly because he first brought them the gospel message so he "birthed" them spiritually. But he is also a father to them in his attitude toward them. He cares deeply for their growth and health and maturity in the faith (2 Cor. 11:28). He doesn't just breeze into town, preach a few sermons, and move on. He invests in them personally, visiting them when he can and keeping tabs on them from a distance when he is away.

What does Paul urge them to do, according to v.16?

Why has he sent Timothy to them (v.17)?

What does Paul call Timothy in v.17?

Two Kinds of Examples

Paul had a good bit of trouble with the Corinthians because they were immature in many ways. One area of immaturity was their propensity toward hero worship. They were quick to forget Paul when a more impressive teacher came to town. Apparently Paul came across stronger in his letters than in person (2 Cor. 10:10). Occasionally a new teacher would come through Corinth with public speaking skills that blew Paul out of the water. Paul was not jealous of the Corinthians' praise or possessive of their attention, but he was concerned that the motives and message of these itinerant preachers may not be entirely pure. And the behavior of the Corinthians implied that these teachers had not been a very good influence upon them. Paul wanted to visit and see for himself what was going on.

Read 1 Corinthians 4:19-20.
When Paul comes to investigate these people of influence in Corinth, what two things about them does he want to evaluate?

What does the kingdom of God consist of, according to v.20?

The Greek word for "word" (or "speech") is *logos*. This means exactly what you would think: speech, words, thoughts put into words. In the biblical context, *logos* means the sayings or decrees of God. Jesus Himself is called "the Word" in John 1 because in Jesus, God has spoken His thoughts to man (Heb. 1:2). When Paul says the kingdom consists of words, He is speaking of the gospel message. There is specific doctrinal content to the gospel. That content must be proclaimed in order for someone to come to the knowledge of God and be born again (Rom. 10:17).

But words are not enough on their own. If the kingdom of God has truly come to a person's life, there will also be power. The Greek word for "power" is *dunamis*. It means force or strength, the ability to accomplish something. Those who have the word of God in power have the ability to act upon it. The difference between false teachers and spiritual fathers is not always evident in the words they speak, but it will always be clear in the example they set.

Words without Power

Jesus once warned His disciples to be careful when following the teaching of the Pharisees. He told them that even though the Pharisees technically taught the words of Moses, their lives did not match their teaching. Jesus said, "…all that they tell you, do and observe, but do not do according to their deeds; for they say things and do not do them." (Matt. 23:1-2) The Pharisees were a classic example of men of words without power.

Paul warned not just the Corinthians but all the churches to beware of men who would come among them with words about God but no power for a changed life.

Read 2 Timothy 3:1-5.
Terrible wickedness is described in v.1-4; but the sobering description comes in v.5. What have these men done?

Now, for contrast, read 3:10-15.
What has Timothy followed, according to v.10?

Verse 13 warns that evil men and imposters will come (as described in v.1-5); but what will keep Timothy from falling prey to them, according to v.14-15? What does Timothy's faith rest upon? Cross reference 2 Tim. 1:5 to see more fully what Paul is referring to.

Paul explains that false teachers will come along teaching things that may sound true, for the most part, but their lives will not bear the mark of the gospel. They will not be men who follow in the footsteps of Jesus and imitate His character of gentleness and humility. They will not look like their heavenly Father in holiness, graciousness, purity, and compassion. They will be the opposite of that. Paul makes it clear that part of evaluating a teacher's words is looking at their character. He urges Timothy to consider the source of the words he hears. Paul is confident that if Timothy does this, he will never be shaken from the truth because the ones who taught Timothy the Word of God were Paul himself and Timothy's mother and grandmother – all of whom demonstrate the power of the gospel in their lives, not just their words.

Words with Power

Not everyone has to learn from their mistakes. Some get it right from the very beginning. The Thessalonian church was one of the fortunate ones.

Read 1 Thess. 1:2-10.
Verse 5 and 6 are the keys to this passage.
In v. 5, how did the gospel come to the Thessalonians?

We know the **word** of Paul was good because he always preached the pure gospel. But, according to the end of v.5, why did the gospel come to them with **power**?

How did the Thessalonians respond (v.6)?

What did they become (v.7)?

What evidence of power did they exhibit (v.9)?

Read 1 Thess. 2:13-14.
What did they receive from Paul?

What did this word do?

In v.14, what did they become?

The Thessalonian Christians were a source of fatherly pleasure and pride to Paul. They followed Paul's example so completely that before long, their fellowship was known far and wide, having become a good example for others to follow. Paul commended them for this.

Paul's Way of Life

Paul was constantly aware of his responsibility to set an example for all believers in everything. As far as he was concerned, if his conduct didn't match his message, his message was negated (1 Cor. 9:27). This is how he lived, and this is what he taught.

Impeccable Discipline

Read 1 Corinthians 10:31-11:1.
What should be our motivation in all that we do (v.31)?

According to 10:33, what was Paul willing to do?

What does Paul tell the believers to do in 11:1?

Read 2 Corinthians 4:1-2.
What has Paul renounced?

How does he live?

Paul would gladly forego any privilege and sacrifice any personal freedom, comfort, or convenience to protect his credibility as a messenger of the gospel. When deciding whether or not to engage in a particular behavior, Paul did not ask, "Is this a sin?" Rather he asked, "Will this hinder my ability to share the gospel with anyone, anywhere, any time?" If the answer was yes, Paul would not do that thing – no matter how harmless it was in itself.

Zero Tolerance

Perhaps because he held himself to such a high standard of integrity, Paul had zero tolerance for any compromise. We have seen how he denounced false teachers for their impure conduct; but Paul went beyond attacking false teachers. When the situation called for it, he did not hesitate to sharply rebuke the Apostle Peter himself!

To understand the context in which Paul did this, you have to understand most of the earliest Christians were former Jews. Many Jewish Christians had a hard time leaving behind the Old Testament laws. Some even felt that the non-Jewish Christians should obey Jewish rules. One of these rules was that Jews were not allowed to eat with Gentiles.

Both Peter and Paul knew that the gospel of Jesus Christ had abolished all the differences between Jews and Gentiles. Favor with God was to come through faith alone, apart from any works of Jewish Law. In fact, to keep Jewish law would actually undermine the gospel because it would make it look like Christianity was a combination of faith and works.

With that background in mind, Read Galatians 2:11-18.
What did Peter (also called Cephas) do in v.12?

What was the result of Peter's actions in v.13?

In v.14, notice Paul's objection to Peter is that he is "not straightforward about the truth of the gospel." The passage does not give any indication that Peter said anything wrong. We can assume his **words** were true and right when he spoke of the gospel. It was in his **conduct** that he was betraying the message of Jesus. To Paul, that was as bad as being an outright false teacher. If Peter had acted in isolation, it would have been serious enough. But this was public; others were being led astray. Paul says, "Even Barnabas was carried away in their hypocrisy." Paul could not stand by and let this happen.

According to v.11, what did Paul do and why?

A Challenge

Most of us are aware that we should be a good example to the lost. We are reasonably careful how we act or talk so that we can keep the door open to invite a neighbor or co-worker to church if the opportunity presents itself. But that is just the most elementary level of the Bible's teaching on being an example. We have a much more important and demanding calling upon our lives: to be an example to our fellow believers.

Each one of us should view ourselves as a link in a chain. We have been Christians longer than some, but not as long as others. In that position, we should be actively following Christ so that we can set an example to "younger" believers with all the zeal and earnestness of Paul. But we should also be observant of those who are "older" in the faith than we are, seeking to follow their example as they follow Christ's. This is the model of growth and discipleship that Jesus set for us when He walked the earth. It is His design for His people and His Church.

Read Hebrews 6:11-12.
What command does the writer give to us?

Read Hebrews 13:7.
What are we supposed to consider before we imitate someone's faith?

A Caution

Unfortunately, we cannot follow just anyone's example. Before we follow in someone's footsteps, we need to see where those steps have taken them. Sometimes we may find ourselves hearing an echo of Jesus' words regarding the Pharisees, warning us to pay attention to a particular teacher's words but not to imitate their actions. Other times we may find that neither the person's words nor conduct are in keeping with the gospel, in which case we have to remove ourselves from their influence.

Ultimately, we should seek to find for ourselves a person who, like Paul, will say to us, "You follow me, as I follow Christ." That person will bring Christ into the 21st century for us, showing us Christ in the context of the modern world, right where we live. That is a tremendous help in our growth as believers, but it must never take the place of our direct imitation of God and Christ. An example is not a mediator. No one stands between us and Christ. Even when we find a good example to follow, our primary role model is always Jesus Himself.

A Calling

Most of us like the idea of finding someone to mentor us in the daily challenges of following Christ. It would be a help and a comfort to have someone ahead of us who has scouted the trail and can encourage and guide us. But that is just one link in the chain. Each of us must also seek with all our hearts to be that example for another believer. Jesus' Great Commission is for each one of us. He tells each one of us to go and make disciples. We are to be like Paul, seeking to "birth" new Christians into this world and then to "parent" them in their Spirit-born life.

The book of Titus makes it plain that the Christian life is practiced in the context of these types of relationships -- older mentoring younger, experience coaching inexperience. This is a natural dynamic, not something we have to plan or structure or force. It begins in the heart of each of us when we truly want to follow Christ. When we want to be like Him more than anything else, we will seek out people who are most like Him and imitate their faith. As we grow to be like Christ, we will find ourselves having His heart toward others, and we will want to reach out a helping hand to those behind us on the path.

Just as Jesus lived each day with one hand clasping the Father's and the other reaching back to His Twelve followers, we will learn to live each day with one hand reaching forward and another reaching back. This is what it means to follow Him and make disciples.

Matters for Prayer

Spend some time prayerfully evaluating your faith. Ask the Holy Spirit to show you if you possess faith in word only or in word and power. If your faith is just a creed and does not seem to include the power to act and change, confess this to God and ask Him to show you what you need from Him.

Ask the Lord to give you discernment to evaluate the "older believers" in your life that have influence over you. If, like the Corinthians, you have come under the influence of men or women who are outwardly impressive but have only the "form of godliness without power," prayerfully consider how you might extricate yourself from your relationship with those people.

Ask the Lord to open your eyes to the "older believers" in your church fellowship who have a faith worth imitating. Study those around you and try to identify the "Pauls" in your midst.

Ask the Lord to cultivate the heart of both Jesus and Paul in your life, so that you would be motivated to take your responsibility seriously to be an example to others. Review the verses we have read about Paul in this lesson and ask for the Spirit to move you toward his level of commitment to Christ and love for believers.

Conclusion

This has been a brief study with a lifetime's worth of application. We have seen a picture of how God intends for us to be – inside and out. He has made us citizens of a right side up and frontwards kingdom in the midst of an upside down and backwards world. He has adopted us into His family, and He expects us to take on a family likeness to Himself – both as God, our Father, and as Jesus, our elder brother. To help us in this process, He has given us the Scriptures in which we find portraits of Christlikeness. In Titus we found several portraits of what Christ would look like in the church, the home, and the workplace.

We have learned that the reason God wants us to bear His likeness is to bring Him glory by adorning the gospel message with the beauty of lives well lived. People will see the truth of the gospel in living color as we obey it and manifest it in the most basic aspects of our lives. We have also learned that those who claim to know Christ, yet deny Him by their actions, bring criticism and shame upon the gospel message and the Savior it reveals.

As we conclude this study, we may feel overwhelmed by the high calling we have received. We may look into our own hearts and despair of ever exhibiting the qualities we have studied. Or we may be excited by the possibilities but unsure of how to get started.

In our first study, *Right From the Start*, we learned that we must fix our eyes on Jesus, the author and the finisher of our faith. We must abide in Him, feed our spirits on Him, and draw our life from Him through time in His Word, in worship, and in prayer. In the introduction to this study, *Keeping Right*, I reminded you that this is not a separate structure. It is another story built on that same foundation. The only foundation upon which to build is Christ (1 Cor. 3:11). Or, to switch metaphors, the only way to be a fruitful branch is to abide in Christ, the vine (John 15:5).

Hearts for Prayer

As we conclude this study, I want to make a final plea for prayer. In Luke 19, Jesus came into the temple and found that it had been turned into a mini-mall. He was overcome with zeal for His Father's house and He literally threw all the vendors out of the temple courtyard. In verse 46, Jesus shouts, "It is written, My house shall be a house of prayer, but you have made it a den of thieves!" According to 1 Corinthians 3:16, our own bodies are now the temple of the Lord because His Spirit dwells in us – just as the Presence of God used to dwell in the temple in Israel. Jesus was angry that the place of prayer had been turned into a place for every activity but prayer. If we are not careful, we are in grave danger of committing the same sin.

Our bodies – our lives – are to be places of prayer. First Peter 4:7 commands us to "be sober in spirit for the purpose of prayer." Ephesians 6:18 tells us to "pray at all times in the Spirit." I think one thing that keeps us from prayer is a fundamental misunderstanding of what prayer is for. We often think of prayer as petition – asking God for things; and that is certainly part of it. But one of the chief purposes of prayer is to put us in a posture of need and dependence before God. Prayer reflects a right view of ourselves in relation to God. It is where we exhibit the humility He wants to see in us before He acts on our behalf. In 1 Peter 5:6-7, we are told to "Humble yourselves therefore under the mighty hand of God, so that He may exalt you in due time, casting your care upon Him because He cares for you."

Prayer tells God, "I need you, and I believe you care for me." That is the message communicated by David throughout all the Psalms. Consider the following sample passages:

"Our fathers trusted in you; they trusted, and You rescued them. They cried to You and were set free; they trusted in You and were not disgraced." (22:4-5)

"A king is not saved by a large army; a warrior will not be delivered by great strength. The horse is a false hope for safety; it provides no escape by its great power. Now the eye of the Lord is on those who fear Him – those who depend on His faithful love to deliver them from death and keep them alive in famine. We wait for the Lord; He is our help and shield. For our hearts rejoice in Him because we trust His holy name. May Your faithful love rest on us, Lord, for we put our hope in You." (33:16-22)

"Taste and see that the Lord is good. How happy is the man who takes refuge in Him!" (34:8)

"The righteous cry out, and the Lord hears, and delivers them from all their troubles." (34:17)

"The Lord helps and delivers them; He will deliver them from the wicked and save them because they take refuge in Him." (37:40)

"Call upon Me in the day of trouble. I shall rescue you, and you shall honor Me." (50:15)

We know that David was a man "after God's own heart." He had qualities that endeared him to God in a special way. David's writings give us a window into the heart that God so prized. These are just a handful of countless possible examples that show us David's total and entire trust in God. David cried out to God constantly. He drew on God's strength night and day. He had an acute sense of his need for God coupled with an unshakeable trust in God's willingness and adequacy to meet his every need.

Isn't this just the kind of response Jesus required from those He rescued from disease? He often asked them if they believed He could heal them, or He told them He was healing them in response to their faith in Him. Perhaps the helpless leper summed it up best when he said to Jesus, "If you are willing, you can make me clean." Jesus replied, "I am willing. Be cleansed." (Matt.8:2-3)

God still seeks those who will come to Him on these terms – faith in His ability and faith in His good character. He wants those who will call upon Him day and night, drawing on His grace to meet their every need. Hebrews 11:6 makes it plain: "Those who come to Him must believe that He is and that He is a rewarder of those who diligently seek Him." Prayer is not just about asking or thanking God for things. Prayer is an expression of a heart-posture of dependence, love, and trust. That is why we are to pray at all times about everything.

Hope in Heaven

The book of 1 Peter would make a great follow-up to Titus, if you want to feed more on the themes that we have been studying. You will find 1 Peter similar to Titus in many ways. We are going to end this study with a look at the "bookends of grace" in 1 Peter.

"Therefore get your minds ready for action, being self-disciplined, and set your hope completely on the grace to be brought to you at the revelation of Jesus Christ." (1:13)

"After you have suffered for a little while, the God of all grace, who called you to His eternal glory in Christ, will Himself perfect, confirm, strengthen *and* establish you." (5:10)

At the beginning and the end of his letter, Peter calls us to set all our hopes upon the grace of God, which we experience now and will experience for all eternity when we are with Him in glory. There are many definitions of grace floating around, but my favorite is John Piper's. He defines grace as "all that God is for us in Christ Jesus." God's grace is all that God gave us when He gave us His Son, who abides in us by His Spirit. God's grace is sufficient for our every need now; but it is also our assurance that the work Christ began in us at the moment of our salvation will be brought to perfection one day (Phil. 1:6). Remember, no matter how feeble our progress in holiness seems to us here on earth, it will be perfected when we see Him face to face; for then we shall be like Him (1 John 3:2). We are to fix all our hopes on this fact and on nothing else.

Our hope for holiness does not rest on our own resources – not on our determination or will power or discipline or even on our amount of knowledge or understanding of Scripture. It is simply "Christ in you, the hope of glory," (Col.1:27). If He is our one hope, then we must fix our eyes on Him. Our one aim in life is to get to know Him now in preparation for knowing Him perfectly when we join Him in Heaven.

Martin Luther said that there were only two days he concerned himself with: this day and That Day. What he meant was that he lived each day of his life with "that day" when he would stand before Christ in view. If we live this day for THAT day, we will realize that cultivating our relationship with the One with whom we will spend eternity is the best use of our time and energy here on earth. Jesus defined eternal life as this: to know God and Jesus Christ, Whom he has sent (John 17:3). According to Jesus, eternal life begins *now* – not "then." This is the hope that should shape our lives.

***Now to Him who is able to keep you from stumbling, and to make you stand in the presence of His glory blameless with great joy, to the only God our Savior, through Jesus Christ our Lord,** be **glory, majesty, dominion and authority, before all time and now and forever. Amen.**
(Jude 24-25)*

For Meditation and Review

Use this page for prayerful review of key principles learned in this study.

Lesson 1: Titus: A Little Book of Big Pictures
- There are 3 kinds of people: those who **do not believe** the gospel; those who **adorn** the gospel; and those who **dishonor** the gospel. My character is the proof of which category I belong to.

Lesson 2: The Kingdom of God: Alternate Reality
- When God saved me, He made me a citizen of His kingdom . The world's kingdom lives for sensual pleasure, judges by outward appearances, and exalts Self. God's kingdom seeks reward in heaven, acts to please God from the heart, and humbles Self.

Lesson 3: Family Likeness: God our Father
- When God saved me, He made me a child in His family. He expects me to imitate Him as a loving child will imitate his father. God's character is holy, gracious, compassionate, slow to anger, and abounding in love and kindness – even toward His enemies!

Lesson 4: Family Likeness: Christ our Brother
- Jesus is not ashamed to call us His brothers and sisters. As our elder Brother, He has set us an example. Jesus is gentle like a sheep (accepting God's will as good) and gentle like a shepherd (tender with sheep but deadly to wolves). Jesus is humble, both in His service to men and His submission to the Father.

Lesson 5: Titus: Portraits of Christ
Christ is & we are to be:
- Sensible
- Sound
- Self-controlled
- Submissive
- Serving faithfully

Lesson 6: Christ's Reflection in the Home
- In her home, the woman is to imitate Christ's qualities of reverence and freedom from gossip or any addiction. She is also to teach what is good – namely to love, to be sensible, pure, a keeper of the home, kind, and submissive to her husband. In so doing, she will adorn and not dishonor God's Word.

Lesson 7: Christ's Reflection in the Workplace
- In the workplace (and in all our work), we are to imitate Christ's qualities of dignity and subjection to authorities. We are to be well-pleasing to those over us, not argumentative, not stealing (even time), showing ourselves to be trustworthy and faithful, no matter who is watching. In so doing, we will adorn the Word of God.

Lesson 8: The Titus Model: A Ministry of Example
- Paul laid down a "you follow me as I follow Christ" model for discipleship. We should have an "older" believer ahead of us and a "younger" believer behind us at all times. This is a great responsibility. We need to be sure that we possess not only the words of the gospel (head knowledge) but the power of the gospel (Holy Spirit's bringing God's Word to life) in our walk of obedience.